Week TO
Strong

Thought-Shifting
Mental Shape-Up Plan

KAT COWLEY

CHANGING LIVES PRESS

CHANGING LIVES PRESS
50 Public Square #1600
Cleveland, OH 44113
www.changinglivespress.com

The information contained in this book is based upon the research and professional and personal experience of the author. Any resemblance to similar ideas, anecdotes, and concepts is coincidental.

Library of Congress Cataloging-in-Publication Data is available through the Library of Congress.

ISBN-13: 978-0-98945-297-7

Editor: Lisa Espinoza
Cover and interior design: Gary A. Rosenberg • www.thebookcouple.com

Printed in the United States of America

10   9   8   7   6   5   4   3   2   1

Contents

Introduction

Our mind and body make for a fabulous team. When both are in prime shape, we perform as the absolute best version of ourselves. The question is, how do we reach this optimal alignment?

According to IDEA Health and Fitness Association, 75 percent of people who physically exercise are not getting the results they want. But of the 25 percent of people who *are* achieving their desired result, **90 percent are working with a personal trainer.**

Apply that same principle to our mental fitness. Similar to personal training in the physical realm, mental training can provide new outlets and a healthy nudge to enhance and reshape your current thought processes.

The secret to a strong and stable mentality regimen:

1. **Make it simple.** Yes, SIMPLIFY your quest into positive territory by breaking it into manageable increments. You don't need a 10-step program or a book that requires a Ph.D. to

read. You are able to change when you see a feasible way to integrate those changes, and finding a relatable outlet makes all the difference. Gravitate to sources you can interpret and identify with on a soulful level. Just as different people relate to different styles of personal training, you may find this book offers the perfect dose of positive mental exercises tailored for you!

2. **Vary your mentality conditioning** by focusing on different thought patterns (mental muscles) you can improve. One week, focus on ways to shift your financial views; the next week, focus on healthy family communication; the following week can pertain to how you view a certain friendship dilemma. Build upon different strengths to balance your state of mind.

As you embark on this 52-week journey, *Week to Strong* will serve as your personal positivity trainer.

Why 52 weeks? That's a long time! Remember—consistency is key. In order to establish new ways of thinking, old habits and patterns must be replaced with new ones. This doesn't happen overnight. But as you consistently engage in the weekly exercises, you will begin to note thoughts and behaviors that affirm you are making progress on your passage toward a more positive life.

Like physical training, your results are dependent on what you bring to the table—partial efforts yield partial results. Aim to dedicate reflection time to each of the weekly segments offered in *Week to Strong*. If you have looked for a structured way to have "me time," this is it. As you turn the page to each new life lesson, take advantage of the contemplation the exercise offers you. Chapters are purposefully short so you can spend most of your time simmering on how you can embody each highlighted life parallel.

Allow a new consciousness to soak it into your life through this lighthearted version of adult story time. Ultimately, you will learn to direct your initial mental responses to a positive place rather than a negative spiral. By imagining yourself exercising love-based thinking in **real-life**, everyday scenarios, you will have the opportunity to contrast how you currently express yourself in each situation *and* be lifted to an alternate view. You will feel better about your responses and about the responses of others toward you. You will gain a sense of everyone being on the same "team" instead of everyone being "out for themselves." Layers of life that once burdened you will be released in the name of inner reconciliation.

Week to Strong is for everyone—whether you are a reflective person who regularly invests in your mental fitness through meditation, journaling, or other avenues, or a curious person investigating the idea of improving your mindset. Even those with the healthiest of mental outlooks will discover new insights about themselves and continue to expand their capacity for a rich, positive-thought life.

I have divine confidence in you as you progress through *Week to Strong*. I predict that each segment will penetrate to your heart's core and plant a seed that will continue to grow and flourish over time. I anticipate that your reactions to discussions or situations will reflect a new, considerate understanding. I look for you to gain a new perspective regarding any negative feelings you have about your current life path. And, perhaps most important, I foresee that you will tap into your positive potential and program it as your *default* mindset.

Keep this book in an eye-catching location so you are easily reminded to contribute to your progress each week. In addition to your own personal work with *Week to Strong,* consider having a weekly conversation with a friend over coffee to process your thoughts, or make a group effort of it. Virtual book clubs are available via the website **www.katcowley.com**. Be creative with how this book can serve you.

May the following insights gift you with a heaping dose of peace, a black belt in the uplifting arts, and a harvest of "I never thought of it that way" moments.

From my heart to your pages,
Kat Cowley

Overcast Ovation

It was a damp, chilly morning, and my inclination was to stay inside and enjoy the warmth of my cozy bed. But I had promised my dog, Mali, a morning beach walk, so I suited up for the cold and possibly rainy weather that awaited us. This was one of those cases where I knew if I'd stop dragging my feet and start moving in the intended direction, I would be glad I did. I was confident that once I reached the coast, all thoughts of staying inside would disappear. The view does that to me—it always manages to leave me breathless the first few moments I try to process it all.

On this particular day, the sky was several shades of gray, and the clouds seemed to spread a layer of lazy dust over everything as they passed. Fewer people graced the shoreline, and the ocean lacked its normal surfer population. The wind and rain had allowed a surplus of seaweed to surface, leaving unsightly patches on the white sand. To the typical eye, it would seem like a "blah" kind of day.

But then I began thinking about how often the typical eye overlooks obscured beauty. Even on that soggy day, sitting amidst the oceanic doldrums, I was able to see the breathtaking view peeking through the gray. The beauty was still present, just in a different package.

Every day is not a sunny one. There will be times in our lives when the people we love and, yes, when we ourselves experience the gray. The exterior may lack luster, and overall energy may be less than vibrant. But look beyond what the typical eye perceives, and seek the beauty that is present even in the gray.

A beach view is still a beach view *even* on a cloudy day.

Each of us embodies bright hues and muted colors. We all possess some gray. Accept your shades—yes, even the darker ones, and allow them their own chance to shine.

This week, embrace your "blah" moments, those times when you may not feel like a "10" or when your mood and energy are on the low side. Choose to let this gray area shine. Embrace the fact you are giving your body some rest as you watch your favorite TV show marathon or spend an entire afternoon in the pages of a good book—in the comfort of your favorite sweatpants—because you don't feel like venturing out into the social world. It's okay to be gray.

Love and accept all of your colors—even the ones you don't feel are your best or that won't invite applause from others. If you can pull off looking good in gray, imagine what a splash of color will do.

DISCUSSION 1

Think about the last time you looked in the mirror and gave yourself a hard time. Maybe it was because of how you perceived your physical attractiveness, or maybe you were questioning the allure of your skills or talents. **There is always something beneath the surface.** Is there a particular person you may be trying to please in your life? Are you playing the "Compare Game" perhaps? When we realize it's really not about how we are . . . it's about the story we choose to believe, we can form action steps toward resolving the real issues. For example, we all have different opinions about what is desirable. Instead of taking this reality personally, liken it to a large group of people ordering dinner at a restaurant. There will most likely be a wide variety of tastes represented, though no one is ordering the "right" or "wrong" item. We simply accept those differences in taste as personal preference. Yet we often become hurt or offended when someone's personal preference contrasts with something we represent. Remember, the "personal" part of another's preferences does not belong to us. We can still be desirable and just not selected for a very impersonal reason.

In what situations have you taken things a bit personally only to realize it had nothing to do with you at all?

⊛ ⊛ ⊛ DISCUSSION 2 ⊛ ⊛ ⊛

What are you grateful for even in the midst of your gray areas? What always continues to shine through your gray?

Personal Dialogue

Enter a very honest place within yourself. Think of the times you may have overlooked, and maybe even rejected, the gray areas of others. Now think of what elements contributed to that judgment. When you are ready to release your judgments of others, you are also ready to accept yourself as you are, disregarding any judgments that are projected onto you in the future.

Keep an account of how you embraced your "gray" areas, as well as the gray areas of others, this week.

SUNDAY

MONDAY

TUESDAY

WEDNESDAY

THURSDAY

FRIDAY

SATURDAY

WEEK

Spare Change

In the past year, I have seen six close friends lose their jobs and one contemplate bankruptcy. Chances are you have encountered your own financial woes at one point or another. During those times, it is easy to give into fear and hop on a merry-go-round of negative thinking.

I was mentally balancing my holiday and monthly expenditures when my mind reverted to the fear that I would not have enough. As I drifted toward the kitchen to get something to drink, my eyes locked on my "ish dish," which holds my keys, business cards, jewelry, and spare change. That's right . . . **spare change**. Spare, meaning extra . . . money that wasn't being used for my immediate survival. My mental state shifted, and I began to focus on being thankful for the "spare change" in life.

No one is immune to financial worry. It creeps up on us and spins a web of uncertainty into our personal lives and mental well-being. But it is important to remember in the midst of that fear that we all have spare change. A surplus. An abundance of some sort. It may be hiding in inconspicuous places, just as literal spare change does, but you have traces of prosperity overflowing in your life—all around you.

This week, take note of your spare change in your car, dresser dish, pant pockets, couch cushions, desk drawer—even the "take a penny" tray at the gas station counter. Let each coin stash renew your security and fuel your gratitude for the surplus in your life.

● ● ● DISCUSSION 1 ● ● ●

Try this exercise to discover the *real* reason for your financial anxiety. I'm giving you a pass to be a pessimist for a minute . . . ONLY a minute. What is the WORST that could happen if you ran out of funds? Would you still be breathing, able to see, walk, eat, touch, learn, and love? Are you actually fearing letting people down or feeling like a failure? When you think about it, would you still have certain friends or family ready to support and encourage you into a new opportunity in life? Many times our fear actually stems from feeling that we would be angrily rejected and left in a lonely state of isolation. Each of these emotional states actually has nothing to do with a dollar sign and everything to do with the value you place upon yourself and the substance of your relationships. In what ways can you improve those two areas?

● ● ● DISCUSSION 2 ● ● ●

Change isn't easy. The financial realm of life has intimidated many of us since we were young and watching our parents manage money. Give yourself permission to take baby steps if necessary toward a new way of looking at financial concerns. Notice when you experience a shockwave of anxiety regarding finances and check in with yourself. *For example:* You are trying hard to manage your finances well, and you receive a friend's destination wedding invitation. You suddenly feel that familiar knot in the pit of your stomach. Take a moment to process your feelings. Sure, it's a bummer you can't make it, but if your friendship is authentic and open, your friend should understand. Instead of focusing on not being able to make the "main event," focus on the reality that you have a friend who thinks so highly of you that they want you to be a part of their milestone occasion. That speaks volumes to the kind of friendship you offer. That thought alone is your "spare change." Think of other examples where you took an inner "time-out" and processed your anxious reactions to various financial situations. What "spare change" discoveries did you unearth?

Personal Dialogue

Tiny Tim was on to something. The best and most authentic way to receive is actually through giving. It has a supernatural effect on our hearts. Consider collecting all the spare change you find and using that toward your own personal Good Samaritan project.

Keep an account of how you encountered different types of "spare change" in your life this week:

SUNDAY

MONDAY

TUESDAY

WEDNESDAY

THURSDAY

FRIDAY

SATURDAY

WEEK

Morning Glory

The online journal *The Clinical Advisor* cited a study that said smokers who light up within 30 minutes of waking are 79 percent more likely to develop lung cancer than smokers who wait an hour before their first cigarette.

What this basically tells us is if a cigarette is at the forefront of your mind *immediately* upon waking up, chances are it will continue to be at the forefront of your mind throughout the day, thus resulting in chain-smoker tendencies and the consequential health hazards.

Now consider this study in terms of our thought lives. The mental vices we entertain within 30 minutes of waking must certainly set the tone for the thought patterns of the day, resulting in negative repercussions in various areas of our lives.

What kind of negative thoughts invade our morning hours?

Ugh, another day at the office! Torture by cubicle.

Guess I need to let the dog out . . . in the rain. Terrific.

I have so much to do today: meetings, a presentation, errands, company dinner, and a piano recital to attend! I can't do it all.

Look at my love handles! It is safe to say I am officially overweight now.

It is freezing! Will the weather ever let up?

Just as lighting a cigarette first thing in the morning leads to a day marked by continuous smoking, so lighting a match to negative thoughts ignites a mental chain of behavior. You are likely to continue the same pattern of thinking for the entire day, then the next, and so forth, until one day a reality check forces you to realize that years of your life were spent in a pessimistic cloud of smoke.

Though some days are destined to be "wrong side of the bed" days, we can still take command of our mental state and aim to devote the first 30 minutes of our day to thoughts that enrich us.

- Place a picture of a positive memory or of someone you admire on your nightstand so you see it first thing in the morning.

- If the weather has you down, make it a tropical morning by listening to your favorite beach-bum tunes and dropping an umbrella in your morning OJ.

- Use sticky notes to post uplifting or funny quotes in areas you will visit often during the day.

- If a stressful day at the office is in store, plan ahead and hit the sack a little early the night before. That way you can get up 30 minutes earlier the next morning and dedicate that time to pampering yourself. Complete a crossword puzzle, read a magazine, or arrange for coffee with a friend. Having "you" time to look forward to will make it easier to give so much of yourself in the day ahead.

● If love handles have you snarling at the mirror, plan recess. If we call it "exercise," it often seems to take on a negative connotation. You *have* to exercise, whereas you *want* to have recess. If you liked riding bikes as a kid, chances are you will still enjoy it! Find a park or neighborhood where you can cruise for some nostalgic activity time. Use the Internet to scour the variety of adult leagues that offer everything from softball to basketball, or email your girlfriends and set up some "walk and talk" times.

This week devote the first 30 minutes of your day to the type of thoughts you want to occupy your mind for the **entire** day. WARNING: *Positive chain thinking is suitable for all ages and may result in good health and happiness.*

✦ ✦ ✦ DISCUSSION 1 ✦ ✦ ✦

Sit and make a gratitude list. Write for as long as the gratefulness flows from you. Place this list in a place where you will see it within the first couple of minutes upon waking (bathroom mirror, microwave door, or coffee pot are good spots). As you wait for breakfast to heat up or coffee to brew, visit your gratitude list each day. Consider it the multivitamin for your mental health.

Feel free to share your gratitude list with a group or your family.

● ● ● DISCUSSION 2 ● ● ●

Think of the top two highlights of your day. Maybe it's your regular daily walk or finally getting to sink into your comfy chair after work. These are positive experiences you've created for yourself. What practice or habit could you incorporate into your life that would help make your first 30 minutes a positive mental space that will influence the rest of your day?

Personal Dialogue

We all have an inner "narrator" chatting away once our feet hit the floor. The great advantage we possess is that we get to select the tone of our narrator each day. If you want to see a scary movie, you're not going to choose Kermit the Frog as your narrator. Likewise, if you want your day to be amazing, you want to avoid a Debbie Downer or intensely critical narrator. Simply think of changing your inner narrator as recasting. He or she doesn't fit the tone you desire to create for your day, so it's your job to replace them.

Keep an account of how you utilized or switched up your first 30 minutes each morning this week:

SUNDAY

MONDAY

TUESDAY

WEDNESDAY

THURSDAY

FRIDAY

SATURDAY

Support Systems

Most of us regularly utilize devices that incorporate auto-support systems of some kind. Whether it is a computer program that automatically saves your work, an alarm with a snooze option, or an appliance that shuts itself off, we each have reaped the benefits of hidden support systems somewhere along the line.

In the same way, our relationships operate as automatic support systems. Whether we realize it or not, there are friends, family, loved ones, and even strangers who are ready to step in and help fill in the gaps when we fall short and need assistance.

Think of a time you sent a card to a friend you knew was going through a rough patch or offered to help a stranger carry their groceries to the car. You were happy to be able to lend a hand or give a word of encouragement. Now remember when you have been on the receiving end of simple human kindness. Someone has put the milk away for you because you accidentally left it out. A stranger found a receipt of yours containing personal information and shredded it for you. Your printer was almost out of paper, so a coworker went ahead and refilled it for you.

There are times when we openly seek out help from others, but each day we are gifted with support we did not even have to request.

This week, be intentional about supporting others before they have the opportunity to ask for help—operate in auto-support fashion. You may never see the reciprocated action, but a network of hidden support will always follow you.

● ● ● DISCUSSION 1 ● ● ●

Recall a time someone (known or unknown) helped you out of a situation without your having to solicit their help or support. How did you feel as a result of their actions? How did their actions change the way you perceived your circumstance?

● ● ● DISCUSSION 2 ● ● ●

Now, think of a time YOU responded in auto-support fashion for someone (directly or anonymously). What feelings resulted from your actions? How did your actions change the way you perceive yourself?

Personal Dialogue

There are times in our lives that we all fall short of time, energy, or expertise. This means each day we can be confident someone could use our automatic support. In what ways could you assist someone without being asked? (This could be as simple as taking the trash out without being asked or scraping someone's icy windshield before they hit the road). What auto-support systems would you like to experience in your own life? Close your eyes and envision a scenario where you are receiving this type of assistance, and invite that support into your life.

Keep an account of how you provided and received auto-support this week:

SUNDAY

MONDAY

TUESDAY

WEDNESDAY

THURSDAY

FRIDAY

SATURDAY

Parking Lot Spots

It is your lucky day! You have successfully nabbed the front parking spot at the grocery store, the bank, and then the dry cleaners. But, as you pull into your office, your excitement begins to wane. You weave through rows of occupied parking spots and find yourself settling on the row furthest from your building. Frustration mounts, the "go figure" attitude takes over, and your previous VIP parking opportunities have been long forgotten.

Life is like a parking lot. Some days you get the spot everyone wants. Other days you have to put in a little more effort and do a little more walking. There are even times you will have to continuously circle until your parking space appears.

The important thing to remember is that *everyone* wants a good spot. So when you find yourself whipping into the front row to nab that desirable space, let it be a subtle reminder of the exceptional blessings life has bestowed upon you against all odds. Out of the entire lot of people just like you, there was a prime spot with your name on it. Your special parking spot is just one of the countless blessings in your life that are remarkably reserved *just* for you.

This week let your parking spots remind you of the effort, perseverance, and moments of gratitude that make up your life.

● ● ● DISCUSSION 1 ● ● ●

Just as we can quickly forget our good "parking spot" fortunes, so it is with the privileges allotted to us in life. What are some of the "front row" opportunities and advantages life has granted you that you may have taken for granted?

● ● ● DISCUSSION 2 ● ● ●

Sometimes traffic can bring out the worst in us. We feel rushed. We are running behind or have a responsibility to fulfill and must stick to a strict schedule in order to get it all done. Here's the thing—we can avoid much of the perpetual hurriedness by leaving 10 minutes earlier than we think is necessary. Ten minutes can literally make the difference in how you drive and treat others on the road. This affects not only your own safety, but also the safety of others. Plus it helps you stay composed instead of morphing into a panicked, finger-flipping maniac. You are more apt to greet passing pedestrians with a wave and a smile than to nearly clip a grandma and her Chihuahua. You will represent the welcomed energy we all enjoy being around and might even make someone's day in the process—all because of 10 minutes.

In what ways can you arrange to add the 10-minute buffer to your departure time? (Get up earlier, drink coffee at the office instead of making it at home, lay your clothes out the night before, or ask for help getting a certain chore done.)

Personal Dialogue

If we are honest with ourselves, a parking war is never *really* about the parking spot (just as road rage isn't really about the road). **It's more about our control of the situation.** If we feel threatened, bullied, in a rush, or in danger, it triggers a reaction in us. Imagine if your sense of calm and composure could bring a blissful balance to an otherwise tense and shaky situation. Like attracts like—if you react with compassion, you will welcome more of that kindness into your lane.

Because getting behind the wheel is such a common act for us, it's easy to forget about the great responsibility that comes with having that set of keys. Part of that responsibility is carrying ourselves in a way that will best serve others on the road or those sharing the parking lot with us. When you get behind the wheel this week, remind yourself how you want others to behave behind the wheel, and hold yourself to that same standard of consideration.

Keep an account of how you acknowledged and expressed gratitude for your prime "parking spot" life opportunities this week:

SUNDAY

MONDAY

TUESDAY

WEDNESDAY

THURSDAY

FRIDAY

SATURDAY

Choosing Your Mental Wardrobe

We are a society that loves to shop. From cars to electronics to clothes, one of our favorite pastimes is searching for and choosing the perfect purchase. What if we threw every single item we saw on the rack or shelf into our cart? What if we exercised no discretion with regard to what we chose to buy and take home with us? Not only would we end up with a whopping bill, we would also end up with a house full of clutter that we couldn't possibly put to productive use. We would find it difficult to locate those items we really needed because of all the unnecessary stuff we allowed to accumulate.

Choosing our mental wardrobe is like shopping for just the right clothes from the rack. Each of us is presented with a multitude of thoughts every minute. *What will the weather be like today? Which outfit will I wear to work? What will I eat for breakfast? Where will I get gas? Which radio station will I listen to? Which lane is better for me to drive in?* The stream of thought never ends. It sometimes feels like we are at their mercy. Thankfully, this is not the case. Like the clothes hanging from the rack at the department store, we can recognize the thoughts available to us and choose only the ones that fit best. Of course, we can also choose to pull every piece off the rack, wear it around, and add it to our pile of mental clutter. Either way, the choice is up to us.

Just as we learn to pay attention to which clothing styles work best for us, we *can learn* to pay attention to red flags our consciousness throws out when we are about to pull some unhealthy or unproductive thoughts off the rack. When you start down a particular line of thinking that has proven unproductive in the past, your mental red flag will resurface. As you become aware of this (and choose to listen to this warning), simply acknowledge the thoughts for what they are and leave them hanging neatly on the rack. Move on to choose a line of thinking that is "in season" (meaning relevant to your day), fits you better, and won't cause unproductive mental clutter for you to sort through later.

Example: Your commute to work

What could be a peaceful, centering time is often the flood-gate to random, mental clutter. *"That car needs a paint job. . . . What did I pay for the last paint job I got? . . . Car shops make a fortune off us! . . . I wish I made more money."*

Whoa—talk about taking a detour. That period of potential solitude was suddenly transformed into self-doubt, all because we pulled some mental clutter off the rack and chose to wear it around for a bit.

The good news is our minds are capable of perceiving thoughts *without actually wearing them around.*

Let's try that morning commute again with a different approach. . . .

"That car needs a paint job." Stop right there and acknowledge the thought as random mental clutter. Ask yourself, "Will this thought tangent help me get on with my day?" If the answer is "no," let the random thought be and simply leave it on the rack. Reclaim your focus, and move right along.

This week, apply the rack approach as you sort through and choose the thoughts you decide to wear around. You will have less mental clutter to sort through and more of the time you crave to just "be."

● ● ● DISCUSSION 1 ● ● ●

Ever find yourself reenacting an unfortunate or even painful situation in your life? Do you sometimes think, "I should have said . . . " or "I can't believe THEY said . . . " So often we push "replay" on scenes we were only meant to live through once. We play them over and over as if reliving them repeatedly will bring closure, when in fact it repeatedly reopens wounds that were in the healing process.

This reenactment routine is one of the ways our mental closet becomes overtaken by clutter . . . and fast. Think about what scenes in your life you are replaying. You wouldn't willingly choose to watch an unpleasant movie over and over again, so don't put yourself through your own toxic performance. When sour memories arise, consider yourself walking into the wrong theater. You wanted to watch *Eat Pray Love* and accidentally walked into *Pulp Fiction* . . . oops. Simply walk out of that theater and into another that is more agreeable to you. Now describe your version of a pleasant mental screenplay. . . .

● ● ● DISCUSSION 2 ● ● ●

Double-team your productivity measures. Go through your "real" closet and clean out any unused or unwanted items. With each piece you remove, consider it a representation of unhealthy thought patterns you are clearing from your mind. Perhaps a bad breakup, a disagreement with a family member or friend, a career move gone wrong, or a lack of judgment resulting in personal anguish? How did this make you feel? Now that you have more room to spare, what items would you like to add to your mental wardrobe?

Personal Dialogue

Like our clothing, sometimes our thoughts just need a little mending. Maybe you have some memories that don't necessarily need to be thrown out of your mental closet completely; they just need a little patching up. Can you think of a situation you can "mend" this week?

*Keep an account this week of how you released
ill-fitting pieces from your mental closet:*

SUNDAY

MONDAY

TUESDAY

WEDNESDAY

THURSDAY

FRIDAY

SATURDAY

WEEK

The Extra Inch

We often hear about people being praised for going the extra mile, but we rarely recognize the power behind a simple extra inch.

I had a roommate who taught me a lot when it came to extra inches. She would always take the extra time to carefully wrap leftovers in aluminum foil before placing them inside a plastic bag. Thus, she would stretch her dollar and spend less time cooking than I did. When it came time to switch from winter to summer wardrobes, she would pack her clothes in a garment bag with dryer sheets, then place them in an air-tight sealed bag. She enjoyed more closet space than I did and less time in the laundry room getting rid of wrinkles and that musty storage smell. As soon as she made plans, whether they were personal or professional, she would immediately sync the appointment into her phone and set a personal alarm to make sure she would not forget. She therefore held a reliable reputation. She used the same method with important dates, so she never missed acknowledging someone's special occasion. If she was asked to dog-sit, she would go ahead and water their plants, so she always got referrals from happy clients. Basically, she was the queen of taking an extra minute to go an extra inch, which made many aspects of her life much easier and more enjoyable.

There are many times in our lives when, despite our best efforts, we simply will not be able to go the extra mile. However, there is not a single circumstance where a simple *inch* is impossible.

This week, find ways to go the extra inch. See how taking a little time and effort reaps its rewards. Whether you accomplish a mile or an inch, it is a step toward rewarding territory.

DISCUSSION 1

What are some "extra inch" behaviors you have noticed in others over the years?

DISCUSSION 2

What are some ways you can add an "extra inch" to duties and relationships in your life?

Personal Dialogue

What really keeps you from going the extra inch in most situations? Is it fear of seeming too eager or your generosity potentially being taken advantage of? Think about what factors might be blocking the extra "inch" from becoming your default setting.

Keep an account of "extra inches" you receive or choose to implement this week:

SUNDAY

MONDAY

TUESDAY

WEDNESDAY

THURSDAY

FRIDAY

SATURDAY

Allow Things That Work for Others to Work

O ne of the primary survival mechanisms we have developed is the tendency to follow our ego as if it is the ringleader of our life. If our ego proclaims something to be true, then it must be true, right? Since we have done such a good job convincing ourselves of this, we naturally try to recruit others to our "right" way of thinking.

The reality is, we each create our own truth based on our *perceptions.* If your perception happens to be healthy, helpful, and enriching—wonderful! Embrace and maintain that truth. But remember that your journey to embrace what is true for you will not be the same journey for everyone else.

When I need rejuvenation at the end of a rough day, I take a leisurely soak in the tub, followed by tasty take-out and a good movie (not going to lie—it's usually an old-school Disney flick). That is my idea of a perfect remedy. However, my best friend would say a trip to the mall for a manicure is the cure-all; my sister would say a lengthy gym session would do the trick; and my dad would proclaim that an afternoon on the mower is the best therapy. What is a privilege to one may be punishment to another. Each of us can have a different perception without interfering with the process of the other. For example, you will not find me trying to convince my dad that a mall is the perfect place for him to relax and unwind.

We are surrounded by people who behave, interact, communicate, and believe differently than we do. We don't need to understand *why* it works for them. Most of us can't fully grasp the theory of gravity, but we appreciate that it works, and that is the important thing. The only process we need to fully understand is our own.

This week acknowledge, appreciate, and celebrate the different ways others navigate their processes in life. You will be surprised at the mental and emotional energy you will regain when you embrace your own truth and allow others to do the same.

⬤ ⬤ ⬤ DISCUSSION 1 ⬤ ⬤ ⬤

Recall a recent time when you questioned someone's belief system or who they chose as their partner, maybe even something as insignificant as what they named their child. Why did their actions really bother you?

⬤ ⬤ ⬤ DISCUSSION 2 ⬤ ⬤ ⬤

Think of the one decision you have made in your life that you are most proud of. Maybe you moved across the country solo or took a chance and started a new business venture. Try to remember the deep sense of pride you have about that choice.

Next time you encounter someone whose decisions reflect a different truth than yours, try infusing their decision with the same sense of pride that you feel about your best life choices. How does it feel to extend that level of respect to others?

Personal Dialogue

When you were growing up, who in your life modeled a judgmental attitude? Did you have a parent, teacher, boss, or close friend who scrutinized and critiqued everyone around them? Go to a compassionate place and imagine why they may have absorbed that nature. Did they want to please a certain person or gain affirmation from a particular group in their life? Stepping into their shoes can bring insight as to why certain judgments arise within you toward others.

Keep an account on how you respected the decisions of others or received respect for your choices this week:

SUNDAY

MONDAY

TUESDAY

WEDNESDAY

THURSDAY

FRIDAY

SATURDAY

Loss vs. Gain

A friend of mine recently lost his mother. Personal condolences began to pour in via text messages, social media outlets, cards, face-to-face communication, and voice messages. Almost inevitably, the first words were, "I'm sorry for your loss."

After hearing that several times, I started to really contemplate the meaning of that phrase, and it occurred to me that "loss" is only one side of the story when someone dies. We often forget to celebrate the other side—the "gain."

Certainly, we do not want to minimize the pain of loss. But we should also remember to celebrate what we gained, how much richer our lives were, because we knew that person. If a person's parting brings tears to our eyes, that just means he or she brought joy into our hearts. We know that the season of time we spent with them, whether two decades or two months, was a gift to us. We were granted two months worth of joy we would have never experienced otherwise.

Your loved one most likely shaped you into the individual you are today. In the good, bad, and ugly, you were constantly being molded into the son, daughter, student, friend, business partner, future spouse, or parent that you are today. They were a tool in that molding and will continue to shape you—just not in the physical form they once embodied. While grief is a natural process, you can be intentional about infusing your grief with gratitude for the time you were given to share with the loved one who has passed. The greatest loss would have been if you had never known them at all.

It has been said that a funeral should be a celebration of life. With sensitivity and compassion, we can help others and even ourselves in times of loss by embracing the reality of sadness but also remembering and highlighting the "gain" side of loss. "How wonderful that you were blessed to share life together," might sometimes be the most appropriate sentiment to encourage someone in one of life's most difficult circumstances.

This week, give thanks for those who continue to add blessings to your life with their presence, while also giving thanks for those who have parted but continue to bless us in their own way. Replace feelings of grief with feelings of gratitude, and don't be surprised if you feel the warmth of their presence surrounding you.

● ● ● DISCUSSION 1 ● ● ●

Think of someone currently in your life who adds a plethora of color to your very existence. You feel more alive when they're around. Think of ways to thank them for sharing their presence—their limited time on this earth—with you. What did you come up with?

● ● ● DISCUSSION 2 ● ● ●

Tap into any feelings of grief you might be carrying. Sometimes we link grief with respect or even homage to our departed ones. Gratitude is both a way of paying respect as well as offering the ultimate homage. Imagine how wonderful they would feel knowing THEY were the reason you have become such a caring parent or talented worker—or seeing that you have a new, fresh outlook on life because of them. Each time you pull one of their wisdom cards from your mental Rolodex, they smile a little, knowing you still remember. In what ways could you allow grief to be transformed into gratitude in your life?

Personal Dialogue

Write a letter to someone in your life who has parted. (Note: grief can be experienced in divorces too.) In your letter, describe all the ways they deposited the best of themselves into you. Close your eyes and imagine handing them that letter.

Keep an account of how you worked to infuse gratitude into your grief while paying tribute to your living blessings this week:

SUNDAY

MONDAY

TUESDAY

WEDNESDAY

THURSDAY

FRIDAY

SATURDAY

Kid Sisters

My friend Jill and my younger sister, Laura, recently visited me in California. As the youngest of three girls herself, Jill began swapping stories with Laura about growing up as the younger sister. When you hear these kinds of stories as adults, they take on a whole new meaning. I suddenly saw through Laura's eyes the importance of allowing a kid sister to join in on a bike ride or slumber party plans. Speaking for myself, back then it was usually out of obligation or guilt that I permitted her to tag along, but from her view, she just knew she was wanted. She was included. She walked away with great memories that she still reminisces about today.

The thing is, all throughout life, we have younger "siblings" who look up to us. While they may not be blood relatives, they are friends, neighbors, coworkers, and acquaintances who enjoy our energy so much that just to be in our presence is a treat for them. Someone you may view as a "pesky little brother or sister" type would love nothing more than to get a phone call from you, be invited to lunch, or be asked to attend a sporting event with you. While it is easy to flow with our normal social circle, embracing them into your plans could result in a day they will remember forever.

This week, embrace the personal compliment of having someone desire your company. Let the joy they receive in your presence fill your day with fulfillment and celebration for the person you are.

My sister, Laura, and me

Shout-out to the little sis. Thank you, Laura, for being an eager (and forgiving) sidekick throughout the years. I can always count on you to be in my corner (and in my stuff). XO

● ● ● DISCUSSION 1 ● ● ●

Think of a time someone you admired unexpectedly included you in their plans. Was it a road trip, dinner plans, or a holiday party? How did their invitation and desire to include you make you feel?

● ● ● DISCUSSION 2 ● ● ●

Think of people in your life who fit the "little brother or sister" role. Why do you suppose they look up to you? How can you include them in your plans this week?

Personal Dialogue

What are the reasons you haven't already included this "little brother or sister" figure? Are you afraid perhaps that they will want to hang out ALL the time? Worried they might not gel with the rest of the gang? Write down any hesitations you have in reaching out to them. With each reservation, write down how you would react should it actually happen. For example, you invite your "little brother or sister" (maybe a new colleague at work) to a friend's BBQ party one weekend. You know your new colleague is a staunch (insert Republican or Democrat), and it just happens that your friends are actively involved with political efforts of the opposing party. Simply inform your friends that you're inviting a colleague who's new in town and that they make politically charged comments from time to time. Then on the way to the BBQ, let your "little brother or sister" know that you appreciate their political convictions, but you think it would be a good idea to avoid any political conversations since your friends are pretty solid in their views, and, after all, this is just a fun, friendly get-together.

Any concern you have can be alleviated by a game plan.

Keep an account of how you included the "little brother or sister" in your life this week. Also think about the qualities you possess that cause others to look to you as an "older" sibling:

SUNDAY

MONDAY

TUESDAY

WEDNESDAY

THURSDAY

FRIDAY

SATURDAY

Build a Castle

O ne of many random side jobs I have done over the years
was assisting an artist who made sandcastles for a living.
She was tasked with designing and constructing a huge sandcastle display for a company that wanted to feature her creation
in their future marketing material. Up until that point, any sandcastle I'd built was from my own imagination, not to any certain
"professional" specifications. So it was interesting to see the
systematic planning that went into the process.

**Surprisingly, most of our time was spent preparing to build
the structure rather than actually shaping it.** We spent what felt
like hours digging a trench at the foot of the castle. We dedi-
cated another hour to tightly packing and then immediately
drenching the sand with buckets of water, over and over again,
to build a firm and even foundation. We were as busy as a Fanta-
sia bucket brigade going back and forth, back and forth from the
ocean to the castle site.

Unfortunately, the tide decided to come in unusually early
that day. I immediately worried we had devoted too much time

to preparation procedures and would not have time to complete the design itself before the tide took its toll.

Turns out, the repetitive shoveling paid off as the tide sunk into the moat's chambers and allowed us to continue building. When time lapsed and water began to overflow the moat, once again my concern shifted to all of our hard work being swept away by the sea.

Again, my worry was unnecessary. Our continuous packing and drenching had resulted in such a solid foundation that the waves pouring over our construction site proved to be no threat. We were able to dedicate another hour to perfecting the details with no problem, and the client could not have been more thrilled by the outcome. It looked as if we had planned for the interruption to take place all along. It then occurred to me that we actually had. What I had thought was a misuse of time was actually an act of strategic preparation.

Sometimes we find ourselves in repeat mode. Our everyday activities become mundane, boring, and even seem like a waste of time. It is not until an unexpected tide arises that we recognize our redundant actions as important steps in a process of preparation.

Something as simple as preparing the office coffee each morning may favorably resonate with an employer during a vital restructuring period. Constantly scrambling to make family dinnertime happen may set the stage for significant conversations that help your child make responsible decisions down the road. Adhering to your morning jogs may one day be the very reason you are able to bypass a serious ailment or complication.

This week, view your schedule in a new light. Applaud yourself for having discipline, perseverance, and structure. Your routine may actually be preparation for the unexpected.

● ● ● DISCUSSION 1 ● ● ●

Can you recount your own "sandcastle" moment that illustrates how your preparatory actions (even if you didn't recognize them as such at the time) paid off?

● ● ● DISCUSSION 2 ● ● ●

Name two routines in your life you often feel are a waste of time. What are some benefits that can emerge from them down the road?

Personal Dialogue

Do you consistently hit rock bottom in certain circumstances? Those situations are excellent opportunities for growth. Think of ways to implement the sandcastle strategy—a strategic plan of preparation—in those areas.

Keep an account this week of how the various routines in your day can eventually serve you down the road:

SUNDAY

MONDAY

TUESDAY

WEDNESDAY

THURSDAY

FRIDAY

SATURDAY

WEEK

Become an Investor . . . of Your Time

alk to anyone who is successful in the stock market, and you will discover that the key to their success is their ability to use time to their benefit—when to buy, when to sell, when to wait things out. Time is a tool they have learned to use effectively.

While we may not all be Wall Street moguls, we can certainly learn something about investing our time wisely.

If you were to ask 10 people what their passion in life was, most would look blankly at you or laugh off the question with a safe answer. Very few people keep the fuel that fires their passion for life at the forefront of their minds, not because their aspirations are empty and of no value, but simply because they haven't managed their time well. You have to make time for things that matter—and your fire for living MATTERS.

It's time to get honest with yourself. Think about this past week and write down the hours you have spent watching television or movies, cruising the Internet, mindlessly shopping, or tinkering with "putter" work. Maybe you took part in a conversation you've already had multiple times.

Now write down the amount of time you spent contemplating your goals for the week, thinking of things you would like to improve upon, exploring your talents, or taking steps to incorporate something new into your schedule.

The point is most people do not even consider reflection on life goals and passions a priority. When we continually choose to forego this kind of self-appraisal in favor of watching YouTube videos or surfing the Internet, we are placing more value on the lives and activities of others than on our own.

Many find Sunday to be a beneficial day for making self-investments. Take a look at what you learned from the week prior, gauge how you are moving toward your goals, and consider how the past week's activities can lead to future growth opportunities. (This is a great jumpstart for your Week to Strong activity!)

This week, start a practice of investing time in self-discovery. Take 30 minutes each week for soul searching that you would normally spend on distractions. We often regret watching a mindless show, but no one has ever said they regretted spending time building their self-worth. Find what really fuels you and construct an action plan of how to attain that goal.

Your life is worth the investment of time it takes to set goals—big, small, short-term, and long-term. Use time to your benefit, and you will reap the rewards of a fulfilling, rich life.

● ● ● DISCUSSION 1 ● ● ●

What are three things you do regularly that you can live without once a week for the sake of investing in self-discovery? (Maybe you could give up a particular social media outlet each Monday or turn your text alerts on silent for an entire evening.) Write your self-discovery time into that slot and document how that week feels compared to weeks where you've taken part in the three "can live without" activities.

● ● ● DISCUSSION 2 ● ● ●

Should you need a little nudge to get you started with your self-discovery, ask yourself the following question: "What feeling do I most enjoy experiencing?"

While we enjoy a lot of feelings, which one is your favorite? Is it when you get a hug of appreciation? That burst of excitement that comes with a new, exciting opportunity? Or recognition for your unique skill set? Brainstorm about what emotion gives you the best "oomph" in your step. From there, create different ways you believe you can consistently produce that feeling. What did you come up with?

Personal Dialogue

What activities summon the "putter" tendency in you? Do you "find" ways to putter around when chores, studies, crunching numbers, or getting your work done calls for your attention? Puttering may seem like a viable excuse to delay your duties, but it really does you a major disservice by postponing the completion of important tasks.

Unearthing and partaking in your life's purpose is your duty. In fact, it's your MAIN duty. When you putter and procrastinate about discovering and pursuing that purpose, you contribute to a sense of complacency that affects the significant goals residing in the deepest part of your soul. Wouldn't you rather do the inner work and enjoy all the rewards that come with being in the flow of your purpose?

Keep an account of how you got creative and substituted "putter" time with important self-discovery time.

SUNDAY

MONDAY

TUESDAY

WEDNESDAY

THURSDAY

FRIDAY

SATURDAY

Putting the "I" in Iceberg

O kay, here's your NatGeo for the day. Think about the fact that 90 percent of an iceberg is unexposed and completely hidden underwater. We see this massive, obtrusive, and yet beautiful hunk of Mother Nature that commands our respect, but far beneath the surface lies 90 percent of what that iceberg is really made of.

And unfortunately, that unseen, underlying mass is what causes ships to crash and wreaks the most havoc.

Our lives are like icebergs. Our actual human presence is only a small fraction of what we are really all about. We consider our external "self" our sole representation because it's what we can see, touch, and know as "real." But far more important are the parts of us beneath the surface—the parts others can't see.

When you interact with someone, remember that what you see is only 10 percent of who they really are. The 90 percent that is unseen represents their character, feelings, desires, and so much more. All the issues they've had growing up, fears they combat every day, rejection they don't want to go through again, apologies they never received, or validation they never got all lurk beneath the surface.

Plato's quote, "Be kind, for everyone is fighting a hard battle," rings true when you think of others in this way. And the "everyone" in that quote includes you. Be kind to yourself when you realize you shouldn't have behaved a certain way, reacted with a particular emotion, or made certain decisions. The 90 percent in you is not easy to identify sometimes either. The important thing is to be willing to feel it and strive to understand it.

DISCUSSION 1

Think of an incidence where you later learned a fact that helped explain why a person behaved or reacted in a certain way. How did that change how you viewed their demeanor or choices?

DISCUSSION 2

Recall a time someone reacted strongly toward you without knowing the "behind the scenes" reasoning for your conduct.

Personal Dialogue

What feelings can you detect beneath your surface exterior? Are they unknowingly causing damage to others?

Keep an account of how you embraced your "beneath the surface" areas as well as those of others:

SUNDAY

MONDAY

TUESDAY

WEDNESDAY

THURSDAY

FRIDAY

SATURDAY

Hear What You See

My friend Ashley told a story about how she bought her little girl, Kallie, a cup of hot chocolate from Starbucks. Kallie wore the biggest smile, feeling so grown up, as she marched around with her "coffee" cup that looked just like mom's.

I'll bet the hundreds of times Ashley habitually drank her coffee, she never realized her actions would register with Kallie on such a level. To Kallie, the cup represented something that was part of her beloved mom's life every single day. Of course Kallie would want in on some of that!

If only we could *hear* what others often see.

People of all ages may not *listen* to what we have to say, but they most certainly *watch* to see what we do. Something as simple as your behind-the-wheel mannerisms, how you recount your day when you come home from work, the way you talk about your friends or significant other, or the hobbies you are involved in touch people around you in either a positive or negative way. Consider how little Kallie silently observed her mom as she cradled her warm coffee cup each day. When the time came for her to finally get a "coffee" cup of her own, imagine how excited and important it made her feel.

This week, think about how your actions are being observed and perceived by others. Chances are you are making more of an impact than you know, and others will find themselves emulating you. Consider how you would feel if you saw someone engaged in a behavior you knew you had inspired.

DISCUSSION 1

Recall two times you emulated someone you respected:
In your childhood or adolescence
In your adult years
Why did they captivate you?

DISCUSSION 2

Recount a time you noticed someone emulated YOU.
In your childhood or adolescence
In your adult years
Why do you suppose you captivated them?

Personal Dialogue

Our society applauds individuality, but part of the road to individuality is sampling what works for you based on what you see and admire. As we grow, our individuality changes based on more desirable features we see and collect along the way. Think of your top three features you admire about yourself as an individual. Where did you collect those examples along the way?

Keep an account of how you provided a positive example this week:

SUNDAY

MONDAY

TUESDAY

WEDNESDAY

THURSDAY

FRIDAY

SATURDAY

Paying Is Giving

Every month we go through the routine of paying the bills. Often unforeseen expenses must be paid as well. Cars need repairs, teeth need crowns, school fees are due, and pets get sick. Let's face it—bills are just as much a part of life as eating and sleeping.

Since their presence is obviously nonnegotiable, why not make bills something you can feel good about? Yes, you read that last statement correctly, and it really is possible to achieve while still in full possession of your right mind.

Let me ask you: What is your profession?

Let's say for the sake of example that you are an accountant. When people have to pay their taxes, you make a living crunching those numbers.

Now let's reverse the role and say you are the individual having your taxes prepared. You are essentially providing for the livelihood of your accountant. Because of you, their car has gas, they have light in their home, and they had something to eat that day. The same goes for your mechanic, dry cleaner, grocery clerk, and even the author of the book you are reading.

The next time you are tempted to cringe at your doctor bill, consider your payment a group donation. Your check will go toward a medical professional paying off years of school loans, an office clerk sending her child to camp, a nurse getting a new set of tires, and a janitor saving toward a honeymoon.

This week focus on all the good that is generated with each purchase. **Turning bills into blessings balances more than just your budget.**

● ● ● DISCUSSION 1 ● ● ●

It would be nice to live in a world where all services were free, or where Skittles was our currency. Since that will never be the case, we might as well embrace the reality that we are all trying to make a living. Think of the last time you paid for something and the purchase price really ruffled your feathers. Think of at least five positive effects that could have resulted from that purchase.

● ● ● DISCUSSION 2 ● ● ●

Think of your current paycheck (or your fantasy paycheck). What if people told you that you didn't deserve it? It would probably sting a little . . . okay, sting a lot. Consider that "sting" feeling the next time you make a fuss over a price point. If you really feel it necessary, how could you express your concern over an asking price in a way that still shows value for the person providing the service?

Personal Dialogue

Think about your answer from Discussion 1. Now pretend someone just handed you a check for $10 million. Would you still be upset about the price tag, or would you nonchalantly pay it without a second thought since you now have plenty of money in the bank?

If you answered "just pay it," you know the price tag was never *really* the enemy. Dig deep. What do you think are your real concerns?

Keep an account of how you embraced the "paying is giving" philosophy this week:

SUNDAY

MONDAY

TUESDAY

WEDNESDAY

THURSDAY

FRIDAY

SATURDAY

Liven Up Your Life

It happens time and time again. We find ourselves in a slump, knowing something's not quite right but not able to pinpoint the problem. No one wants to be unenthusiastic about life.

The thing is, drastic measures are not always the answer. Oftentimes all it takes to break our habitual tendencies and revive our outlook is a small dose of pizzazz. Try switching up your cabinet space. Place cups, plates, and utensils in different areas for a fresh feel to your kitchen. Replace your shower curtain with something funky to brighten your morning. Rearrange your furniture and artwork around the house or your workspace. Make up your bed in a new fashion or switch the side of the bed you sleep on. Replace your old standby brand with something different (detergent, shampoo, milk, etc.). Smells also enhance our mood. Consider a unique scented candle you can enjoy. Start a new morning ritual like switching the news to a different channel or drinking a new flavor of coffee. Commute to work using an alternate route, and listen to a different type of music than you typically gravitate to. Place something atypical on your desk. Even something as insignificant as a new haircut or ring-tone on your phone can add a bit of zest to the day.

Every day we engage in activities driven solely by habit. By simply replacing or reviving minor patterns, we can resuscitate our oomph and our attitude.

This week consider how some of your habitual activities could be opportunities to incorporate fresh elements or new changes into your life.

● ● ● DISCUSSION 1 ● ● ●

As you read through the various ways to switch up your habits, did you feel inspired to make some small changes? What creative pick-me-up ideas did you come up with?

● ● ● DISCUSSION 2 ● ● ●

Think of someone in your life who is down in the dumps. Is there some small change you could suggest that might energize their day?

Personal Dialogue

Making changes to our physical appearance can certainly make a difference in how we experience life. But small changes on the inside can make a significant difference, too. Is there an area of your personality that could use a little adjustment? For example, if you feel you might be a little too shy for your own good, challenge yourself to be the first one to introduce yourself in a group setting at least once in the next week.

Keep an account of how you livened up your life this week:

SUNDAY

MONDAY

TUESDAY

WEDNESDAY

THURSDAY

FRIDAY

SATURDAY

Answer with Questions

When someone asks us for advice, it's an immediate ego booster, right? It gives us a sense of authority and intelligence. It is very tempting to begin spouting off our ideas and opinions as if we are the resident expert regarding the matter at hand. Next time your advice is solicited, try answering their questions with more questions.

Often when faced with a dilemma, we already know what our decision should be—we just want validation of our choice from someone we trust. With this in mind, think about how you could be most helpful to your advice-seeking friend. For instance, suppose they ask you if they should take a new job. Respond by asking some thought-provoking questions. "If this were the last job transition you would ever be able to make, would you still take the job? Can you see this job falling into place with you personal life in a couple of years? What are you most looking forward to about this new job? What assets will it contribute to your daily life?"

The most effective teachers know how to ask well-crafted

questions that point *toward* the answer rather than handing their students a solution. You can use this same technique to point others toward their own best path.

This week resist the urge to give directions to others. Let the questions flow and watch as the pieces fall into place and they arrive at a place of clarity. You may even find answers to your own questions in the process.

DISCUSSION 1

We all have the best of intentions, but sometimes we give, and get, plain old bad advice. Think of a time when it would have been more helpful had your request for advice been met with thoughtful questions instead of suggestions. What questions do you think would have steered you in the right direction?

DISCUSSION 2

Think of someone who frequently comes to you for advice or a listening ear. What are some questions you can ask them in the future that could provide valuable guidance?

Personal Dialogue

Why do you usually seek advice? Is it because you're unsure what to do or because you want validation that you've made the right decision? Write a series of questions to use next time you find yourself at a fork in the road. Your questions may very well uncover your own best advice.

Keep an account of how you gave guidance with questions instead of answers this week—for yourself and others:

SUNDAY

MONDAY

TUESDAY

WEDNESDAY

THURSDAY

FRIDAY

SATURDAY

Freedom Through the Phases

Nothing in life stays the same. Relationships, circumstances, desires—everything changes. We all move through various phases in life. The question is, do we give ourselves and others the grace and freedom to move through these phases in our individual ways?

I had a friend who was struggling in her relationship. She eventually came to the conclusion that her partner was not a bad guy; he just wasn't a good guy for her. I was thankful she was able to see the situation for what it was—neither of them was right or wrong. They had simply gone through phases of change, and they were no longer right for each other.

This is also the case for a lot of friendships and professional relationships. There is constant friction because of contrasting personalities. Think of an earthquake: two tectonic plates decide to maintain different levels, and catastrophe ensues.

Remember being content to play in a sandbox, and suddenly your playmate decided the sandbox was for "babies"?

When your idea of Friday night fun was pizza while watching your favorite TV shows, and your older sister would not be caught dead with you at home? When your summer vacation was spent surrounded by friends, and then your best friend decided a romantic getaway with their honey was the ultimate retreat instead? Maybe you can recall the last office karaoke Christmas party before it became too hard for coworkers to get a babysitter? Or when you decided it was time to gravitate toward a new social circle during a divorce? In each of these circumstances, no one is wrong. They just represent different phases of life.

This week, be respectful of the shifts occurring in your personal life, seeing them as periods of growth that require some time to play out. Allow yourself and others the freedom to develop who they are at this point in their lives. They will welcome and appreciate your support.

● ● ● DISCUSSION 1 ● ● ●

Recall a time you were in a different life phase than your friends. In what ways could you have used their support? How can you offer that same encouragement to others who may be in a different life phase than you right now?

● ● ● DISCUSSION 2 ● ● ●

Think of a time you unknowingly caused an "earthquake" by trying to hold on to someone who was shifting phases. How can you avoid a repeat disaster in the future?

Personal Dialogue

What is the root intention you have for holding on to someone? Do you love their presence or fear the void should they move on? Get deep and uncover why it might be hard to let others shift phases. (Reverse the exercise and ask yourself why others may be desperately holding on to you.)

Keep an account of how you embraced the shifting of phases this week:

SUNDAY

MONDAY

TUESDAY

WEDNESDAY

THURSDAY

FRIDAY

SATURDAY

WEEK

CATastrophe?

I was a houseguest of a friend in college when absolute disaster struck. I accidentally left the front door open wide enough for the roommate's cat to seize its opportunity for a great escape.

I quickly recruited my fellow road-trip warrior to help me scour the woods for the fleeing feline. We endured thornbushes and poison ivy, tripped into a sinkhole, and called for the cat until we were just about hoarse. We emerged from the woods empty handed and looking like we belonged in a Stephen King movie.

My face stained with tears, I trudged back toward the house with my friend, disappointed that our fun roadtrip had turned into a lengthy animal search-and-rescue mission. As we neared the front door, there was the cat lying contentedly on the welcome mat.

I realized the cat was never really lost, only at recess. Its freedom had ironically caused my fear. It is all about perspective. While the cat's great escape represented danger, death, and sorrow to me, it was actually just a chance for the cat to chase a few rodents, mark some new territory, get some fresh air, and climb a few trees. Hardly the danger zone I automatically envisioned.

This week, remember that fear can obscure our perspective and diminish our freedom. When your mind jumps to the worst-case scenario, redirect yourself to focus on potential positive opportunities. **Your catastrophe could very well be your gateway to freedom.**

● ● ● DISCUSSION 1 ● ● ●

Recall a time you reacted to an incident fearfully only to discover later that the circumstance was beneficial in your life.

● ● ● DISCUSSION 2 ● ● ●

When have you been the "cat" in this story? Everyone around you thought the sky was falling, and you remained as cool as a cucumber amidst the chaos. What caused you to maintain composure?

Personal Dialogue

What current area in your life are you viewing with "catastrophe" lenses? Imagine at least two freedoms that could be hidden inside those challenges.

Keep an account of how you reframed your "catastrophe" lenses so that they became freedom lenses this week:

SUNDAY

MONDAY

TUESDAY

WEDNESDAY

THURSDAY

FRIDAY

SATURDAY

Energy Feed

You know how there are people who walk into a room and the party officially starts with their presence, or how lunch was not the same during school when a particular friend was home sick? Perhaps the office feels a tad stuffy when the boss's spouse comes to visit, or you suddenly feel uneasy when a certain relative drops by.

It is all about energy.

Try an experiment: Put your hands palms down while a friend places their palms face up. Place your hands as close together as you can without touching. Maintain that stance for a minute and you will soon feel the heat from the other person. That is basically what body heat is, the transferring and receiving of energy from one person to the next.

The thing is, an assortment of energy is being transmitted constantly around us. Just as we physically feel the energy from body heat, our consciousness picks up the energy others bring with their presence, and our emotions react to it.

Do you ever wonder what type of energy you bring to a

room? Do you bring a compassionate, warm, fun-loving vibe, or do you bring a little black cloud with you?

The good news is we are in total control of our energy output, and we can also exercise a large degree of control over what kind of energy we receive. By receiving energy from positive forces in our life, we are able to give off similar energy to others.

This week, make it a point to surround yourself with your "A-game" friends. Plan a lunch date, Skype session, or phone chat. Visit a place that conjures that feel-good sensation, whether it is a certain restaurant, bookstore, coffee shop, or your grandmother's house. Wear the outfits you usually save for special nights out, and make plans to cook your favorite dinner while watching your favorite movie one night. The abundance of uplifting energy you absorb will no doubt be passed on to others you come across in the week ahead.

⚬ ⚬ ⚬ DISCUSSION 1 ⚬ ⚬ ⚬

Who is your top "good energy" pick? What do they consistently bring into the room when they enter? What do they add to the conversation flow? How do you think they sustain that type of positive energy?

⚬ ⚬ ⚬ DISCUSSION 2 ⚬ ⚬ ⚬

What are at least two things you bring into the room when YOU enter? What are two things YOU add to the conversation flow? What is one thing you would like to add to that list?

Personal Dialogue

What would you say is your little black cloud attribute? What step can you take toward eliminating that part of your energy?

Keep an account of how you received and transmitted good energy this week:

SUNDAY

MONDAY

TUESDAY

WEDNESDAY

THURSDAY

FRIDAY

SATURDAY

Understand Your Dynamic

Our reactions are a direct result of our experiences. You might be terrified of the dentist because as a child you were on the receiving end of a painful, botched cleaning attempt, and now anxiety strikes when you smell latex gloves. Likewise, whether it's a response to a crying child, an unruly teenager, a loud neighbor, or a heavy workload, it is shaped by our experiences.

In every situation you encounter, some dynamic from your past influences your response. So learning to get to the root of your reactions can yield great benefits for you and for your relationships.

For example, you just had a fight with your significant other for being on their phone during dinner. Sure, it is inconsiderate and poor etiquette, but your reaction seems out of proportion to the situation. You feel such a strong sense of disappointment that you either inflict the silent treatment for the remainder of dinner or you spew out an array of hurtful words.

What was the spark that fueled that fire? A little reflection time might uncover that when you were young, your parents frequently put work and their affairs before you. As a result, you allowed yourself to believe those things were more important to your parents than you. Unwittingly, your current partner's actions simply revived a suppressed and accumulated hurt. Now that you have uncovered your dynamic, you can unravel the knot it has left inside of you for so long. Explaining this to an understanding partner can pave the way for many peaceful dinners to come.

This week reflect on your reactions. What prompted a tear from a playful remark or embarrassment from a joke? Did negative feelings surface over something that really was not a big deal? Did something mundane cause waves of stress? **When we learn to explore our emotions, we use our reactions to our benefit.**

● ● ● DISCUSSION 1 ● ● ●

Think of the last time someone's actions elicited a strong reaction from you. Why do you think it had such a powerful effect on you? How can you weaken the connection between your painful past and the present moment?

● ● ● DISCUSSION 2 ● ● ●

Have you been on the receiving end of a hypersensitive reaction lately? Does sifting through your own sensitivities enable you to offer a bit more empathy and compassion?

Personal Dialogue

When we have unfavorable experiences, they are designed to teach us some sort of lesson. What experience do you repeatedly find yourself responding to in a touchy manner? What lesson could all of these repeat occurrences be trying to teach you?

Keep an account of how you analyzed the root of your sensitive reactions this week:

SUNDAY

MONDAY

TUESDAY

WEDNESDAY

THURSDAY

FRIDAY

SATURDAY

Meet More Plane Friends

It's quite common to hear stories of how couples and friendships formed on airplanes. Their stories strike a chord with us because they're a tangible example of destiny. Out of the millions of places these two people could be, they selected the same flight out of dozens of airlines, and end up in neighboring seats out of 200 some odd possibilities. The stars seemed to align in an undeniable way.

While it may be easier to strike up a "plane" friendship because, let's face it, you aren't going anywhere (on land that is) for a while, potential friendships wait to be discovered in a multitude of ordinary places *every day*. Destiny is just as much at play in a doctor's office, in line at the post office, or on an elevator. The people we encounter in all our daily routines are just as likely to become "plane" friends, as they too were placed in our proximity amidst millions of other possible coordinates.

Imagine if we gave off that same "available" impression in our day-to-day activities as we do when we board a plane and sit down beside another fellow traveller. What if we did not have a cell phone glued to our ear or our fingers busily responding to text messages? What if we did not live every moment in a hurry with places to go and things to do? How many "plane" friendships have we bypassed due to our "busy" vibe?

This week run errands free of tech devices and distractions. **Clear your mind to the best of your ability and put yourself at ease to create an approachable vibe.** You will be surprised at the faces and interactions you will take notice of and how strangers suddenly possess a different appeal. Remember, many of the people you now cherish were once strangers, but you made yourself available so that destiny could take its course.

● ● ● DISCUSSION 1 ● ● ●

What are your usual "go-to" diversions when you are waiting? What is a more approachable position you can assume? For example, if you occupy yourself with a book, people are apt to ask what you are reading or comment on the fact that they've read it too. My mom loves to crochet baby beanies for a newborn charity, and people often start conversations with her based on their unique interest in crocheting. Even reading a newspaper can start a current events dialogue.

● ● ● DISCUSSION 2 ● ● ●

Describe how you met at least two treasured individuals in a "plane friends" kind of scenario.

Personal Dialogue

Why do you believe you put off the "busy" vibe in certain social situations? Do you feel uncomfortable if you are not constantly occupied? What do you believe is the root of your unease? How can you take steps to conquer your fear of not being busy?

Keep an account of how you embraced opportunities to make "plane friends" this week:

SUNDAY

MONDAY

TUESDAY

WEDNESDAY

THURSDAY

FRIDAY

SATURDAY

Soul Medicine

A friend of mine was venting about her boyfriend's golf habits. There was a social gathering she had wanted them to attend as a couple, and she finally convinced him to bypass his golf game that weekend. The next weekend, her parents unexpectedly came into town, and she felt it was important he spend time with them since they were anxious to get to know him better. Now there was only one remaining weekend in the following three weeks that he could reserve for 18 holes, and wouldn't you know that weekend it rained—hard.

Her boyfriend began acting differently than usual. After several needless arguments, my friend finally realized that she had essentially robbed him of his "medicine." While it might not be her remedy, golf was medicine to his soul. He gained a sense of relaxation, healthy competition, personal challenge, and enjoyment of friends and nature during his time on the course. Golf was not an escape from her or their functions as a couple. It was a vital part of his life that brought balance and a release from the stresses of the week.

If someone were sick, you certainly wouldn't deprive them of their medicine or ask them to run a marathon. We encourage those feeling under the weather to take care of themselves.

The everyday stuff of life can make us feel under the weather emotionally, and even physically. So it's important that we take our medicine—the antidote that safeguards our sanity, our spunk factor, and gets us back in the game. And it's important to allow the people we care about to do the same. Maybe your medicine is getting your hair done, buying a new outfit, surfing, or gardening. Everyone has their own brand of soul medicine.

This week, resist the urge to judge another's soul medicine.

● ● ● DISCUSSION 1 ● ● ●

Recall a situation where you judged someone's soul medicine. Why did it bother you?

● ● ● DISCUSSION 2 ● ● ●

What kind of soul medicine do you take every now and then? Describe how it improves your life.

Personal Dialogue

Try putting aside any material soul medicines you may consume (pedicures, shopping, or a treat at your favorite bakery), and engage in a more natural form of medicine—a long walk, journaling, watching a sunset. Compare the results you experience with both material and natural soul medicines.

Keep an account of how you or others benefitted from "soul medicine" this week:

SUNDAY

MONDAY

TUESDAY

WEDNESDAY

THURSDAY

FRIDAY

SATURDAY

How Bad Do You Really Want It?

I once read an article about a celebrity mom of newborn twins in which the reporter expressed surprise at the fact that the superstar mom took the 3 a.m. wake-up calls on her own rather than delegating those duties to a live-in nanny as so many other celebrities did. The mom went on to rave about how much she adored those times. For years she had prayed to become a mother, and now she reveled in not one but two answered prayers. I could not help but smile at her new fortune. I took personal satisfaction in knowing that someone who desired motherhood that much was able to reap its rewards.

It made me think about how sometimes the more unappealing elements of life (such as screaming 3 a.m. wake-up calls) can cause us to resent things in our life that we had once desperately hoped for. For example:

When you find yourself complaining about the job you once crossed your fingers for, hoping you would make it to the next round of interviews.

When you skip classes in college after all the financial sacrifice and academic effort it took to get there.

When you feel like you are "over" your partner and forget all the times you prayed they would call for that first date.

The new mother was able to find joy in a seemingly unpleasant task simply because to do so meant she was living out her dream of being a mother—something she had desperately longed for and now treasured so dearly.

Dig within to discover what you want versus what you really need. **Life wants to bless us by granting what we need for our highest good, not clutter our existence by fulfilling half-hearted desires.**

This week, note areas in your life that may be unfulfilled. Ask yourself, "If I attained my wish, **even on the worst of days**, would I be happy?" Perhaps something you *think* you want is actually a representation of another area needing attention. Realizing the difference in the two could bring forth an entirely different desire.

● ● ● DISCUSSION 1 ● ● ●

We all have to give a shout-out to unanswered and unmet desires. Recall at least one thing you desperately tried to call into your life only to later be immensely thankful for the disregarded plea.

● ● ● DISCUSSION 2 ● ● ●

Describe something in your life you wanted so badly that even on the worst days, experiencing its fulfillment inspires that "Ahh, you gotta love this!" feeling.

Personal Dialogue

What is that ONE thing you want to usher into your life? What are some reasons the request could be on hold or simply not in the works? When you compare this desire to your answer in Discussion 1, do the desires have anything in common?

Keep an account of how you analyzed and came to peace with any unmet desires this week:

SUNDAY

MONDAY

TUESDAY

WEDNESDAY

THURSDAY

FRIDAY

SATURDAY

Experience Consciousness

We often use the term "self-conscious" to describe something we are insecure about—our age, weight, complexion, economic standing, or social skills. We all possess a soft spot that is a sensitive subject. Unlike the soft spot on the tops of our heads at birth, the soft spot with regard to our self-consciousness is something we develop at some point based on our life experience.

I once taught a daycare class, and to this day I remember each of my kids distinctly. Children are a walking reminder of how life is rooted in purity. I might have taught some of them how to tie their shoe or spell their last name, but they taught me more than they will ever know.

It was in watching them interact with one another that I decided "self-consciousness" could just as aptly be called "experience consciousness." Children do not know what ugly, fat, poor, old, or weird is until someone describes it to them. Based on their experience with hearing those words, they develop experience consciousness.

When you looked in the mirror as a four-year-old, you did not notice your ski-slope nose until someone made a hurtful remark about it. You were not "self-conscious" at all. You looked at your reflection and were completely satisfied until an experience marked you otherwise.

Think of your current soft spots. When did they develop? At camp when you were young—in high school or college? From a joke told at an office picnic one year?

One of the hardest things to do as humans is to resist the temptation to absorb the projections other individuals place upon us. Think of it this way: if someone thinks the color blue is awful, do you get rid of all your blue possessions? No! You simply take that as their personal color preference. The same goes with our experience consciousness. You could have dated someone who thought freckles were your most adorable feature, and your experience consciousness would admire that trait upon each reflection. That same reflection might be viewed differently had their projection been different. **Either way, the only "self-conscious" act was when you allowed yourself to buy into someone else's perception of you.**

This week, remember that you were once completely unself-conscious. You once looked at your reflection without a single insecurity. Reconnect with that part of your persona and disconnect from your experience consciousness.

● ● ● DISCUSSION 1 ● ● ●

Memory Lane Road Trip! Describe an affirmation you received in childhood or adolescence from someone that caused you to feel secure in a particular area today. What if instead of an affirmation for that particular aspect of who you are, they had expressed a form of disapproval? How would you feel today?

● ● ● DISCUSSION 2 ● ● ●

Think of two people you HIGHLY admire and respect. Now, think of at least one way you pride yourself in differing from their personal preferences. (For example, your mom swears by a certain brand of laundry detergent and you enjoy using a different product. Or your best friend loves redheads, but you're a brunette kind of person.) Why do you think you are comfortable with those preferential differences and not with others (such as looks, career choice, or belief systems)?

Personal Dialogue

Think of what you are the MOST "self-conscious" about. Perhaps you'd never admit this to another soul as long as you live. Can you change your perspective to embrace the reality that your soft spot in this area really stems from a case of buying into someone else's preference?

Keep an account of how you identified and reconstructed your thinking around areas of "self-consciousness" this week:

SUNDAY

MONDAY

TUESDAY

WEDNESDAY

THURSDAY

FRIDAY

SATURDAY

WEEK

License to Fly

Fact: Orville Wright did not have a pilot's license.

Obviously, the man credited as the *first* person to fly an airplane did not need a license. With so many American's actively revamping their resumes, this is important to remember. You could very well become a revolutionary character in your desired field simply because you invent it.

I think of how my résumé once promoted my work as an event planner. To the reader, I appeared by all accounts to be the perfect candidate. I had the education and extensive experience to go with it. It seemed anything from academic to sport to corporate functions I could handle with flying colors. Truth be told, when I was in college and scouting for internships, I picked the fun ones. I wanted a part in the Chamber of Commerce golf challenges, free seats to sporting events, and to play with the animals at the zoo while having a part in seasonal functions. Time marched on, and I kept accumulating new gigs based on networks from previous events. I was an "Event

Planner" before I knew it. The ironic part is, I don't like to plan. I am the most sporadic person ever! Not to mention, I don't stress over specifics, so paying attention to intricate details is not my forte. You will hardly find me in a tizzy worrying about which color napkin to place on tables or proper wine pairings.

As most of us are aware, you can only keep up your ruse for so long before your true colors begin to bleed through. Slowly but surely, I would get pulled into the boss's office for a "talk" on my lack of attention to detail. My gig was up. No longer did I want to funnel my energy and fight frustration on a job that didn't allow me to apply the gifts and talents I could bring to the table.

While I may not be naturally gifted in structured, detail-oriented positions, I am naturally gifted in creative roles. It was then I realized that there were writers out there with similar "looks good on paper" prestige who actually didn't love to write! My, my, we are some conflicted creatures.

I decided I was more interested in roles that not only allowed but also *encouraged* my actual skill sets. Looking good on paper to meet someone else's expectations only pays off for so long. In what other ways could you be de-energizing your own desires while playing this type of smoke-and-mirrors game?

When you soul search and discover the role you were meant to fulfill, do not let the list of things you can't put on a résumé hold you back. Orville Wright never had a pilot's license, yet he's the one in the history books.

This week, reinvent your résumé. It's not what you haven't done; it's what they haven't seen yet.

● ● ● DISCUSSION 1 ● ● ●

In what areas do you bring an undeniable flair or expertise? Can you elaborate on ways to turn that gift into a job skill? For example: You always start the conversations that get people engaged at dinner parties. People want you to sit at their table! You could add "natural connector" to your repertoire. Think of ways your personal characteristics can be repurposed into résumé lingo.

● ● ● DISCUSSION 2 ● ● ●

Is there something you *can't* put on your resume that is holding you back from pursuing your aspirations? How can you utilize the Orville Wright method and create a different road to that goal all together?

Personal Dialogue

The truth is, the standards of a "normal" résumé are constantly changing. As a challenge, start integrating one "outside the résumé box" tidbit on your resume or online professional profile that introduces a potential employer or client to your unique personality.

Keep an account of how you "reinvented" your special offerings to the world this week:

SUNDAY

MONDAY

TUESDAY

WEDNESDAY

THURSDAY

FRIDAY

SATURDAY

Table for Teddy?

Our cell phones have become the adult version of the teddy bear. We tote them around wherever we go and feel safer in their presence. We play with them, dress them up with fancy covers, buy them cool accessories, and teach them app tricks. They even eat with us and often sleep beside us on the nightstand. We sure do love our telly bears.

One morning at breakfast, I saw a dad do something that really spoke volumes to me. He took his kids' and his wife's cell phones as they ate together and placed them in a cell phone pile at the corner of the table. As I looked around the room, I noted table after table where couples and families were enjoying quality time—with their telly bears, not with each other. But this one dad knew the surefire way to get his family to focus on one another was to eliminate the opportunity for digital distraction.

Just as you had to be reminded to keep the video game in the car during your sister's choir recital, it wouldn't hurt to carry over the same "stash it" philosophy with your cell phone. Sure, they are fabulous devices that help us stay connected in positive ways. But when you ask for a table for two, make sure it is just the two of you (you know, humans). Your phone did not rsvp.

This week, think of your phone as a teddy bear. You would be embarrassed to lug a stuffed animal to your dinner table and talk to it throughout the meal. Not to mention how humiliating it would be to receive a pricey traffic violation for talking to a teddy bear instead of driving responsibly. Accept that your phone does not have to be your constant companion. Your phone may help you prioritize your life, but it should not take the place of your true priorities.

● ● ● DISCUSSION 1 ● ● ●

What are your feelings about cell phones and personal interaction with others? What cell phone etiquette do you appreciate from others?

● ● ● DISCUSSION 2 ● ● ●

It's easy to give ourselves the "in case of emergency" excuse for constant telly bear companionship. But remember, children were raised and commutes were successfully taken before the invention of cell phones. What are some ways you can break the constantly "checking" habit? What are some ways you can feel "prepared" without relying on your phone to save the day?

Personal Dialogue

How much time do you spend with your telly bear? Are you a habitual social media, email, or text checker? Perhaps you whip out your phone as a "busy prop" during the lull or awkwardness of wait times. Sometimes it's hard to imagine that we can successfully operate detached from our devices.

Arrange for an **entire day** this week when you can stash your phone. (Leave a voicemail greeting saying you are taking a one-day cell sabbatical, and let your family/friends know you will be out of pocket that day if needed.) Describe how you felt on this day. How did you fill your "waiting" gaps? Did you feel more connected to yourself and your environment when you were disconnected to your device?

Keep an account of how you weaned yourself from your telly bear this week:

SUNDAY

MONDAY

TUESDAY

WEDNESDAY

THURSDAY

FRIDAY

SATURDAY

Symptom vs. Fear

There comes a time when we all hit rock bottom. We find ourselves constantly down on our luck and in the rut of a lifetime. It is usually in these moments of desperation that we pray for our situations to change. Little do we realize, what we really want is for the *fear* rooted beneath the situation's surface to be removed.

Personal example: I highly value my independence. My mom laughs about me being the kid tripping on her shoelaces because my constant refrain was, "No, let ME do it." I've always felt secure when I can take care of and provide for myself.

You can imagine my panic when I was laid off from my job a couple of years ago. My personality changed due to my internalized stress and fears. I would inwardly plead for "the path that leads me to the right job." I continued that inner petition for months before I realized I was thinking backward.

Not having a job was only a *symptom* of the real problem, and finding the right job was not the cure to my inner turmoil. I needed to address the true problem—my fear of having to

106

depend on others. I began to ask for peace throughout the process, that I would surrender the reins, that my mind would be free from anxiety and fear of judgment from others and myself. **Peace was immediately restored once I realized the root problem and stopped focusing on the symptom.**

The financial symptoms suddenly started taking care of themselves. Someone would give me a gift card they said they would never use themselves, or I would land a gig that would pay the amount needed to cover a certain bill. I discovered a cash bonus on a credit card from the previous year that paid off an entire month's expenses. Stocks I did not even know I had were brought to my attention. It was revealed to me time after time that finances were never the problem—my willingness to analyze my fear was.

This week, think about the answers you are seeking. Have you been addressing symptoms? Look at the emotions beneath the surface and find the root of your uneasiness. Enjoy the freedom, comfort, and peace this honest evaluation offers you.

● ● ● DISCUSSION 1 ● ● ●

Bandages don't heal cuts; they just cover them up. What go-to bandages do you regularly use to try to fix life's cuts and scrapes?

● ● ● DISCUSSION 2 ● ● ●

Common fear flairs include not enough time, money, know-how, ability, or appeal. What are some examples of root beliefs that are hidden beneath the surface of those doubts?

Personal Dialogue

Recall a time in your life when you were especially panic stricken. If you were able to go back in time and tell yourself how things would end up playing out, how would that have changed your demeanor during that phase? The next time a potentially stressful circumstance emerges, imagine your future self paying a visit and assuring you that this too shall pass and everything will be all right.

Keep an account of how you uncovered the roots of particular issues instead of focusing on symptoms this week:

SUNDAY

MONDAY

TUESDAY

WEDNESDAY

THURSDAY

FRIDAY

SATURDAY

Applause Starters

We have all been at a movie theater or a performance of some kind where someone starts to applaud, and soon the entire crowd is clapping. Sometimes the initiator even stands up, and you watch the ripple effect as some people automatically (and others more reluctantly) stand in unity.

I remember one time seeing a man stand up to clap only to find that no one joined him. Since that was the only time in my entire life I had witnessed that scenario, it made an impact. Once he realized no one else was going to stand up, he kept clapping until he felt he had paid due homage to the speaker (or at least had somewhat saved face).

There is an *automatic* applause and an *authentic* applause. So many of our actions in life are actually *reactions*. Our thought processes seem to be on cruise control as we assume our actions in mechanical fashion. Do you find yourself saying, "Thank you," "Please," "You're welcome," or "Love you," with no thought as to what the words really mean? That is our automatic applause response. We are supposed to say those things so we follow suit with the expected gesture.

This week, be an applause starter in life. Give a genuine "Thank you" to those who perform well in life. You do not have to wait for Secretary's, Veterans, Mother's/Father's Day, or your anniversary to show your appreciation. Instead of automatic applause, offer the authentic kind. Even if you stand alone, you stand as a genuine fan that performer will always remember.

● ● ● DISCUSSION 1 ● ● ●

Recall a time someone gave you a gift, card, or act of kindness when it wasn't a special occasion—only because they appreciate you. How did that authenticity affect you?

Now recall a time you knew you were receiving "automatic" applause (think unenthusiastic servers singing you Happy Birthday). How does accepting that kind of applause differ from your earlier example?

● ● ● DISCUSSION 2 ● ● ●

Describe someone who you feel deserves an authentic round of applause. How could you plan to verbally praise them or offer a gesture of gratitude this week?

Personal Dialogue

Our society often doles out compliments or excess praise in the name of politeness. (Think of welcoming a guest with, "Oh, what a lovely fragrance!" when in fact the smell made you gag.) While wanting to uplift others is an honorable intention, attempt to save your praise for admirations you authentically connect with this week in particular.

Keep an account of how you practice authentic applause instead of automatic applause this week:

SUNDAY

MONDAY

TUESDAY

WEDNESDAY

THURSDAY

FRIDAY

SATURDAY

Human Petals

If you'd like a therapist but can't afford one, Mother Nature is free of charge—and comes highly recommended. Each day you can spot an endless array of natural wonders that make for grand soul sessions if you look around with open eyes and an open heart.

Take a flower bud, for example. You look at it and know that it is a flower (in training). One day, it will be in full bloom and full color, with an amazing aroma to go with it. One day. . .

If you were to see the flower bud and think to yourself, "You know, I really want to see this flower, TODAY," and started prying apart the petals one at a time, what would happen?

That is the very same scenario we sometimes find ourselves in with the people in our lives. You know there is so much beauty waiting to be displayed. What is holding up the "blooming" process?

Well, nature isn't on our time clock, and neither is the rest of the human race. Things take time. Some flowers, like Zinnias, take only six weeks to bloom, whereas the Century Plant takes 23 years to bloom (and actually only blooms right before it dies).

It certainly is tempting to tug on someone's personal petals. We can rationalize our intervention with, "Just this one little tug and it will all start to unfold . . ." But it doesn't work that way. The process needs its due course.

Enjoy the excitement and curiosity of our human blossoming process. When the bloom comes around, it will be in life's perfect timing, or season if you will, and worth the wait.

DISCUSSION 1

Can you recall a time someone tried to "pull" on your petals? How did that affect your developmental process?

DISCUSSION 2

Mother Nature truly is one of the best therapists in town. Describe a "session" with nature that has enriched your soul.

Personal Dialogue

Is there someone in your life on whose petals you might be tugging? What is one way you can help support them this week during their blooming process?

Keep an account of how you supported yourself and others during life's blooming process this week:

SUNDAY

MONDAY

TUESDAY

WEDNESDAY

THURSDAY

FRIDAY

SATURDAY

Losing Hair

I overheard a father comparing photos from his oldest and youngest daughter's weddings. At that moment, he realized how much hair he had lost over the years. Right there before him was a stunning visual confirmation that in a period of five years, he had lost over half of his follicle following.

It is the gradual effect that sneaks up and shocks us in the end. Think of the millions of hair strands we have on our heads. Losing a couple dozen each day is no big deal. Each day you look at yourself in the mirror, and you seem to be just the same as the day before. It is not until we look at pictures from the past that we realize how the mirror fails to portray the significant changes that are moderately taking place over time.

Our behavior and thought patterns operate in the same fashion. Letting a bad day become a bad "two days" seems harmless enough until we see that our sour attitude is taking its toll on those around us. Giving in to thoughts of inadequacy on one project makes it that much easier to discount your talents on the next venture. Allowing yourself to partake in one juicy tidbit of table gossip will soon lead to a constant craving for the talk of the town.

One strand of hair lost is not a big deal. The dramatic difference is a result of repetitive loss. When little by little you consistently allow your personal belief system and self-esteem to be chipped away, you will soon find that you have become a different person in the mirror altogether.

This week, look at your reflection and think back to who you were five years ago. Now remember the dad's reaction when he looked at his daughters' wedding photos. Have you realized you are gradually losing a part of yourself? Spend a little extra journal time this week uncovering elements you want to preserve and celebrating aspects you may have brought into your life in recent years that have improved you as a whole. Aim for making sure that when you look in the mirror, you will be proud of your inner reflection—today and five years from now.

● ● ● DISCUSSION 1 ● ● ●

Surprise yourself by the difference a lapse in time makes. Think of a personality trait that you have developed within the past five years. What new trait would you like to embody within this upcoming five-year window? Why did you choose this particular trait?

● ● ● DISCUSSION 2 ● ● ●

It may seem intimidating to release or gain a personality trait, but we do it all the time. You may have once been shy but released that trait after moving several times as a teenager, taking public speaking classes in college, or joining a community group where you were constantly meeting new volunteers and fellow community leaders. Now people actually describe you as outgoing. Had you never experienced the moves, the classes and the group functions, you might still be a shy person.

What are some steps you can take to integrate your new desired trait from Discussion 1?

Personal Dialogue

Is there a trait you have taken on that you wish to release? The dad may not be able to go back in time and get his hair back, but we are blessed with the ability to change the story of our life at any given moment—and this includes rewriting our behavior and disposition. Release that temperament and replace it with the new trait you'd like to embody from Discussion 1.

Keep an account of how you created opportunities to integrate your desired new trait and how you worked to release any unhelpful traits this week:

SUNDAY

MONDAY

TUESDAY

WEDNESDAY

THURSDAY

FRIDAY

SATURDAY

WEEK

Portion Control

Many of us are blessed to live in an environment where food and drink are easily accessible. We can even eat and drink to our heart's content. After hosting some breakfast guests, I emptied my coffee pot into the sink thinking to myself, "Did I really need to make that much coffee?" It's easy to fall into the "better too much than not enough" mentality even with the trivial decisions in life. We tend to think we need more than we really do.

Day after day, we fill our tubs and showers with enough water to bathe entire families in other cultures. We scrape remaining courses off our plates because our eyes were too big for our stomachs. We have so much excess that we actually employee "Waste Management" squads to collect it on a *weekly* basis.

Do you really need a 30-minute shower every day? Can you cut your computer browsing by 15 minutes? As good as mom's chocolate pie is, do you really need three pieces? And will the lights left on in your bedroom help you read when you're out in the living room?

This week, practice being conscious of your consumption—food, utility usage, time allotments, purchases, etc.—and take a portion *from* your portion. You will find you are not only saving money, nixing extra pounds, helping the planet, and becoming more resourceful, but also discovering a newfound satisfaction and soulful appreciation for the generous portions you have been allotted in life.

DISCUSSION 1

Small changes are still changes in the right direction. Something as trivial as vowing to unplug your charger once your devices are charged is a quick and easy habit to pick up. Several coffee shops now offer reusable cups and give you a discount on all future cups of coffee on top of that. Can you think of another quick fix in the portion department? Imagine how many wonderful changes would ensue if each person adopted one quick portion control change.

DISCUSSION 2

Potlucks are a wonderful place to practice portion control. Trust me, I know the feeling of seeing your grandma's pie and having inner taste bud turmoil try to convince you TWO pieces is what you need. Yes, two. Load up. Practice identifying your real needs and tending to them rather than catering to illusions of what you think you need.

What is an illusion need you are creating right now even though your life plate is full?

Personal Dialogue

What are some occasions in life that trigger your "need more" reflex? Write a list of all such incidences. Now revisit Week 25 "Experience Consciousness." Can you see ways your experience consciousness has shaped your misconception of needing more or overindulging? Perhaps you overspend when shopping because you are "experience conscious" that if you don't wear the right designers, your colleagues will not take you seriously in your line of business. Combine the philosophy of this week's highlight with Week 25 and see what revelations emerge.

Keep an account of how you embraced respectful portion control in areas of your life this week:

SUNDAY

MONDAY

TUESDAY

WEDNESDAY

THURSDAY

FRIDAY

SATURDAY

Share Yourself

Someone shared with me how a Vietnamese coworker conducted a native Friendship Tea ritual in their office. The pot of tea had a flower bud inside that they all watched unfold and expand before their very eyes. When the flower was prominent in all its glory, they each poured a cup and enjoyed the Friendship Tea together. Had their coworker never shared the tea ritual, they would have missed out on that unique experience.

A similar "sharing" occurrence happened one day as I admired the view at a local surf spot. On a neighboring bench was a dad with his young son in his lap. The dad was pointing at all the waves and describing the surfer lingo for each of them. His little boy repeated the wave jargon and watched as each wave formed, playfully shouting, "Whoa!" as each one hit its peak and crashed. I realized the dad was sharing himself with his son just as the coworkers had shared themselves in the office that day.

Our individuality is such a gift, to ourselves *and* to everyone around us. We could have been designed to look, think, and act the same way. Imagine what the world would be like if we had the same meals, fashion sense, religion, and hobbies. Someone along the way brought a bit of red into your life, another blue, another green, and so on. When we share ourselves, like the coworker or the man on the beach, our colors come together to make a brilliant combination.

This week, become an artist in your own sense. Add a bit of color to the lives of others by sharing your passions, knowledge, insight, and what makes you—You.

● ● ● DISCUSSION 1 ● ● ●

Recall a time someone shared part of their uniqueness with you and how it left an impression on you.

● ● ● DISCUSSION 2 ● ● ●

What can you share with others this week? Did your father teach you a car-repair trick you can show your friends? Is there a particular workout routine, travel trick, holiday tradition, recipe, or meditation you can share with someone?

Personal Dialogue

Chances are you might have thought a bit on Discussion 2. It's easy to get tripped up and think, "Well, what could I possibly offer people?" But the fact is, you bring your own vivid shades to the world. If you need tangible proof of that, just think of other members of your family and how different you are from them. The combination of those differences is your unique shade.

If you had to consider yourself a color, what would it be? Just for fun, look up what energy that particular color represents. For example, after thinking about my characteristics, I felt my shade was orange. When I looked into what orange symbolized, I found: *Orange combines the energy of red and the happiness of yellow. It is associated with joy, sunshine, and the tropics. Orange represents enthusiasm, fascination, happiness, creativity, determination, attraction, success, encouragement, and stimulation.**

The description you get will be a good start to help you brainstorm on what you bring to the table. With the first three words of that description alone (joy, sunshine, tropics), I realized that I embody the beachy, sunny side of life vibe. I can walk into a conversation that is heading down pessimistic pike and steer the discussion in an upbeat U-turn onto the sunny side of the street without people even realizing they just hit a detour.

What did your color description conjure in you?

Note: This information came from www.color-wheel-pro.com/color-meaning.html

Keep an account of how you embraced your unique shades as well as those of others this week:

SUNDAY

MONDAY

TUESDAY

WEDNESDAY

THURSDAY

FRIDAY

SATURDAY

Skiing Scared

A handful of times I have found myself on top of an icy mountain surrounded by skiers and snowboarders. While this is many people's idea of paradise, one of my ultimate fears lies here—where heights and potential collision unite. Each time I agree to make the trip, I really believe this time will be different. I will suddenly demonstrate agility and confidence on the ice. When I actually arrive at the top of the hill, my illusion is shattered along with my tailbone. The thing is, I fall on my own accord. Not once has someone ever actually crashed into me. I panic that I cannot control my actions and wipe myself out. Not to mention, I put myself at a greater risk of injury because I am so tense.

On one of my "landings," I sat and looked at everyone around me. There were four-year-old kids whizzing past me, while others were hitting jumps and spraying snow as they maneuvered with ease. People were having fun while I was having a panic attack, but we were doing the exact same thing! Or were we?

At that moment I recognized the difference. Their mentality was enabling them to have an experience of self-assurance, challenge, time with friends and family, enjoyment of the outdoors, and above all, fun. My mentality was focused on one thing only—survival. I wasn't enjoying any of their playful perks. I was solely concerned with preventing injury at all costs.

If that was the root of my thinking, no wonder I was skiing scared.

How many times have you skied scared in life with your relationships, career, aspirations, and social dynamics? When it looks like everyone else is having a good time and you're not, you might need to ask yourself that very question. Perhaps you have been hurt in the past due to tension in your approach. It is one thing to believe "this time" things will be different but quite another to make choices toward real change so that history will not continue to repeat itself, resulting in more unpleasant hard "landings" than you'd ever want to experience.

There's a purpose for the bunny slope, just as there's a purpose for taking baby steps in life. One courageous foot forward is all it takes to begin experiencing your encounters differently.

● ● ● DISCUSSION 1 ● ● ●

Is there a situation in which you find yourself "skiing scared" all too often? What is the root mindset causing that inner panic? When you look at those without your level of anxiety, how do you think their perception might be different so they are able to operate without doubts?

● ● ● DISCUSSION 2 ● ● ●

Think of a "skiing scared" situation you have already overcome. How can you apply that victory to the situation in Discussion 1?

Personal Dialogue

Often our exposure to certain elements makes all the difference in whether we fear or embrace certain circumstances. For example, I wasn't exposed to skiing until I was a teenager, while others were on skis at age three. How do you think your upbringing might be affecting your anxiety from the situation in Discussion 1?

Keep an account of how you reevaluated various "skiing scared" situations in your life this week:

SUNDAY

MONDAY

TUESDAY

WEDNESDAY

THURSDAY

FRIDAY

SATURDAY

Wear with Care

If you're reading this book, chances are you are someone who thinks positively or at least is trying to think positively. Bravo!

As you've probably come to learn, when you are on the positive path, there will be plenty of people who come along to try to divert your direction. Sometimes it's because they are lonely on their not-so-cheery path or because they have a case of jealous jitters. Or maybe they don't even know why they are intent on bumbling up your day—they're just mad, okay! Life has its way of sending party poopers our way to test our inner resolve to remain positive.

As year after year goes by, I find myself with a consistently high happy-meter. Sure, I still have grumpy days, but they are far and few between, and I actually find myself benefiting from the solitude and reflection time those days offer. I'm not a millionaire; I'm not famous; I don't hold any titles or records; I've never been invited to the White House; and *Vogue* doesn't have my phone number. But—WOW—have I got a GOOD life! I've learned to recognize all the highlights in my life, and that brightness overflows into my attitude and interactions with people. The result is a general disposition of happiness.

It's easy to let our happiness meter dip depending on the conversation we're in. If the other person exudes a "one day closer to the weekend" vibe or they sigh repeatedly during the convo, we can bet they aren't having a stellar day. It can be tempting to let ourselves sink down with them. But why let go of our positive outlook because of their experience?

This doesn't just happen with individuals. Peer pressure happens in groups as well. We sit around a table and try to fit into the flow of conversation. If the group is upbeat, we try to match that level. If they are complaining, we nod our heads and shrug our shoulders in agreement.

Imagine you have a designer outfit that looks amazing on you. If Sally dropped ketchup on her outfit and was bummed about it, would you smear some on yours too? Or if Bob shrank his pants in the wash, would you throw yours in the dryer on high heat to shrink them too? No, you'd be proud of your outfit and would take special care to keep it in good-as-new condition. If you'd cut a hole in a pair of Dolce & Gabbana shoes to help someone else feel better, I need to seize your closet immediately.

Think of your persona that way. Don't shrink yourself to fit in. Take care of that wonderful designer attitude. If that means limiting time with certain people, coordinating a new lunchtime so you have a different crew to dine with, or pre-brainstorming lighthearted topics that leave little room for the "Blah!" zone, then so be it.

Each time you leave your level to make them "feel comfortable" on theirs, you're not doing anyone any favors. They are already uncomfortable—that's why they are complaining. You are essentially high-fiving their uncomfortable status. It's the same as seeing someone who is mad because they are out in the rain and deciding to step outside with them instead of pulling them indoors with you. And take note: if there are people in your life who like to connect in a "downer" fashion, think about what their role is in your life.

Wear your persona with care. It is truly a priceless design made just for **YOU**.

● ● ● DISCUSSION 1 ● ● ●

If you went out to eat wearing your amazing designer outfit, you would protect your lap with a well-placed napkin. In the same way, sometimes we need protection for our persona. What are some ways you can protect your persona from getting "dirty" around certain downer types in your life?

● ● ● DISCUSSION 2 ● ● ●

Have their been good times in your life you were afraid to bring up because you didn't want anyone to think you were rubbing it in? Or perhaps you felt a bit guilty that all this "good" was coming into your life? You kept all those beautiful vacation pictures to yourself, didn't mention your latest promotion, or mummed the word that you were getting a new car?

When the unworthiness wheel starts spinning, thoughts creep into your head like, "Well, [so and so] is a much better person than me and has had it so rough," or "Lots of people in this world don't have this opportunity."

You have what you have because life specifically **gifted** it to you. When something good happens to us, we commonly use the word "blessing" to describe that particular grace. Now really think about the word "blessing." YOU were blessed. YOU were selected for that particular ray of abundance. You were handpicked to receive a gift in life's custom-made section. And like all custom-made gifts, you didn't get it by accident. That coaster set didn't just "happen" to have your initials on it. And likewise, life did not mistakenly present you with your endowment either. It was a purposeful exchange. Life is the giver. You are the recipient. Never be ashamed of the way life chooses to pay tribute to you.

So if your honey surprises you with a cruise to Jamaica, don't feel bad that you are the only one in your family taking a vacation this year. If you land the promotion over a coworker who has been there five years longer, there's a reason for that. And if you find yourself the primary breadwinner because an extra set of zeroes found their way to your paycheck, that money is being placed in your hands for a reason as well.

Gifts come to you in their perfect time, when you are the perfect recipient. Let any shame associated with your newfound blessings be replaced with a simple statement—"I was **chosen** for this blessing. Thank you."

Take a couple of minutes to share any blessings you would like to vocalize. This is a free-for-all in verbal gratitude.

Personal Dialogue

It can seem tricky to share good news with downer individuals. Sometimes it's just a phase they need to go through, and we need to respect that. Other times their perpetual negativity is a signal that it's time for you to integrate new people into your support circle.

One of the best places to find support is to locate a group or organization that specializes in your passion: a sport, theater, animals, photography, writing, traveling, exercise—you name it! This is a great way to find people who have positive energy toward the same things that excite you. Being able to share that positive energy will go a long way in keeping your day-to-day disposition sunny-side up. What is a positive outlet you can investigate this week?

Keep an account of how you embraced your "designer persona" and helped others rise to that level this week:

SUNDAY

MONDAY

TUESDAY

WEDNESDAY

THURSDAY

FRIDAY

SATURDAY

The Rear View

It was one of those days that was too beautiful to stay indoors, so I decided to put my walking shoes on and take my dog, Mali, on a hike up to the mountain behind our house. And when I say hike, I *mean* hike. I'm a power-walker to the max, so it's always full steam ahead if you're with me.

Well into our hike, I began to get pretty tired. I just kept reminding myself that the view from the top would be worth it and kept trudging onward—picking up a pooped pooch once in a while to give her a break.

Poor little Mali finally had enough. She did one of her "halt" moves where she lies down surrender style. I picked her up and carried her to the side so we'd be out of the way while we took our break. It was when I finally sat down that I looked at the view behind me. It was breathtaking. I wasn't at the top, but this view alone was worth the hike. The scene was so panoramic that my camera couldn't capture all the good stuff in a single shot. I could see where the skyscrapers of downtown San Diego met the bridge to Coronado Island, and I could see the rest of the islands out in the distance past the shoreline. Several sail-

boats coasted in the bay areas. I could see the beach and all the different piers, the houses on a hill, and the mountains capped with snow in the distance—I could see it all.

I realized this was a metaphor for our drive to the "top" in life. We get so busy plowing ahead and creating forward momentum that we often fail to appreciate the amazing things in life that are already a part of our view.

This week, I'd like to encourage you to stop and take a look at what you have already achieved, created, gained, and prospered from in your life thus far. You may find your current vantage point already contains the view you were seeking all along.

● ● ● DISCUSSION 1 ● ● ●

What are some aspects of your rear "view" that you might not be acknowledging due to your full-steam-ahead predisposition? How can you appreciate your current "view" this week?

● ● ● DISCUSSION 2 ● ● ●

Think of all the "little things" that make up your scenic view on a physical hike. The village of small mushrooms, dancing dragon-flies, a squirrel zipping in and out of a hollow log—each of these creations is its own miracle. Seriously, think of the magnitude of creativity engineered within a butterfly—and chances are we see at least one of these mystical creatures each day!

Make a list of all the cunning creations you notice in a new light this week and imagine how it would feel to describe their existence to someone from another world.

May you embody a new infatuation with all that surrounds your scenic view.

Personal Dialogue

Have you ever gotten to the peak of one of your life ambition "hikes" only to find that you apparently climbed the wrong mountain? Perhaps a lack of judgment disguised as a relationship or opportunity caused you to veer off your original course at some point. There are even cases when we may let another individual who is so excited about their "peak" persuade us into thinking their path will also lead to our outlook of fulfillment.

Regardless of how you lost your way, the view was nothing like you expected and you immediately felt as if all that time and energy went to waste. Reflect on two thoughts:

1. Can you pinpoint where and why you veered off course and how you can apply that knowledge to your future life ambition "hikes"?

2. What is a lesson you learned or blessing you walked away with that serves as a nice parting gift for this "peak" detour situation of yours?

Keep an account of how you acknowledged the greatness that is a part of your current life "view" this week:

SUNDAY

MONDAY

TUESDAY

WEDNESDAY

THURSDAY

FRIDAY

SATURDAY

It's All In
How You Wear It

Watch any fashion show and you will see models clad in outfits that would have garnered some curious glances had you worn them to the supermarket. As they march down the runway, it's clear they are able to pull it off because of how they wear the outfits—confidently.

While I was both appreciative and excited, I still remember being mortified to drive my dad's hand-me-down older model car once I turned 16. I prayed no one would see me as I arrived at school, sporting events, or parties. When I would meet new friends, I always dreaded having to point out my car as we walked into a parking lot.

It was not long before a friend of mine inherited her own hand-me-down car, and it was just as much of an embarrass-ment, if not more so, than mine. The difference was in how she drove it. She pulled right up to the front parking spot if it was open. She would offer to give everyone a ride since her car was so big. She gave it a funny name, and before we knew it, her out-of-date ride had become the friend caravan. I was thankful for the lesson my friend taught me. She did not feel any shame, so no one else thought there was anything to be shameful about. I soon found myself embracing my "Gray Bomb." Lots of great memories (both life-threatening and fun) were made in that car thanks to my new outlook.

It's all about emotional intention. If you see the experience as a time to let your self-assurance and spunky side shine, you will emit a totally different persona than someone who sees the experience as a chance to impress others. One intention is to share yourself; the other is to compare yourself. How you present your personality has everything to do with which intention is holding the reins.

If you are comparing instead of sharing, you may think your talent and skill set are not up to par. In that case, someone who might be less equipped than you will take the prize solely because of their confidence levels. If you have something to say but feel too inhibited to say it, someone else will speak up before you and get their request because of their gumption.

This week resist the temptation to think others may somehow be "better" than you. No one was created with secret ingredients. We are each purposefully created for our own brand of greatness. When you see someone who presents themselves in a way you find appealing, remember it is their intention and confidence that gives them the edge. Practice setting your own intent and watch your once timid experiences change for the better.

● ● ● DISCUSSION 1 ● ● ●

What is something you are currently self-conscious about? What is one way you can create a more lighthearted vibe around that insecurity? For example, you have a very small house compared to your friends. You could host a "Tiny Tim" party one holiday season. It could very well end up being the most fun your friends have all year—and create a whole new perception about your home.

● ● ● DISCUSSION 2 ● ● ●

What is a something (a trait, disability, or setback) that you currently wear confidently? Where do you think that assurance is rooted?

Personal Dialogue

Think of ways people throughout your life have thrived and attracted others because of their magnetic disposition in otherwise limiting areas of their lives. For example, your childhood next-door neighbor never had any of the "fun" toys other kids had, such as a video-game station, a large movie stash, fort, pool, or trampoline—yet their home is where everyone wanted to go play. Your neighbor was great at inventing games out in the yard or playing pretend. Even though they didn't have a treasure trove of store-bought amusements, they knew how to bring fun to the table. What other ways have you seen individuals operate with similar magnetism?

Keep an account of how you confidently "wore" your identity this week:

SUNDAY

MONDAY

TUESDAY

WEDNESDAY

THURSDAY

FRIDAY

SATURDAY

Cart Boy Charisma

I recently found myself with extra time on my hands awaiting a cake order at a local grocery store. With a paper, coffee, and donut in hand, I situated myself at a picnic table outside the double doors.

It wasn't long before my attention was captured by a fine young man: the cart boy. Adorned in his florescent orange vest, this young man with apparent developmental challenges proudly marched throughout the parking lot in search of the next stray cart. He would peek down each parking row as if he were a kid approaching a Christmas tree after Santa paid a visit. I watched as his smile broadened each time he discovered his hidden treasure on wheels. Upon returning each cart to the rack, he'd pat the front of his vest and say, **"Good job!"** as he continued in his next cart pursuit.

I teared up thinking of how pure he was. Then I thought of how great of an example he was to us all. Not only did he find joy in a job most of us would grumble over, but he was also so proud of himself. His accomplishments were certainly praiseworthy.

How often do we fail to give ourselves credit? We downplay our personal accomplishments, thinking that they aren't actually good enough to warrant praise. *It wasn't a big deal. Anyone could do it. So-and-So did something twice as impressive.* Sound familiar?

Your assignment this week is to consciously congratulate yourself each and every time you do something good—no matter the level of difficulty of your accomplishment.

If you hold a door open for someone, mentally declare, "How nice of me!" If you arrive to work on time, award yourself another "Way to be accountable!" salute. Give yourself props for going the speed limit, biting your tongue in a confrontation, paying your bills on time, finishing household chores, or wrapping up the last chapter in the book you've been reading for the past month.

Let the mental applause roar when you help someone find something they lost or send a friend a lead that lands them a job. Your self-respect will continue to rise as your self-directed kudos continues. When your habit is to constantly commend your endeavors, **you become your own best promoter**.

The next time you find yourself with a shopping cart in tow, think of all the self-encouragement you can fill it with. Much love to my favorite cart boy for inspiring this wonderful reflection.

● ● ● DISCUSSION 1 ● ● ●

Name three things you did yesterday alone that are praiseworthy. (Simple things count too!)

● ● ● DISCUSSION 2 ● ● ●

Have you ever witnessed your own version of "cart boy charisma"? Share what you learned from that person's example.

Personal Dialogue

It's funny how we can rattle off a list of what we believe we did wrong during the day but fail to remember anything we did right. If we can be our own worst critics, why not instead become our own biggest fans? As silly as it may feel, pretend you are the official president of your own fan club this week. Think about how fans treat the people they admire—they think *everything* they do is fabulous! Even if their idol makes a mistake, they remain loyal. Give yourself that degree of admiration this week. Cutting yourself some slack and offering a personal pat on the back can go a long way in bolstering your self-worth. Not to mention, you will begin to recognize the praiseworthy actions of others as well.

Keep an account of how you gave yourself surplus praise this week. This is your official BRAG SHEET:

SUNDAY

MONDAY

TUESDAY

WEDNESDAY

THURSDAY

FRIDAY

SATURDAY

WEEK
39

Appointment Please

We make appointments for just about everything these days. From car repairs to school conferences and lunch dates, our agendas are the anchor to our sanity sometimes. While it is tough to feel like the majority of your day is planned before you hit the floor, you can rest assured your day will be far more productive when guided by an overall sense of direction. Otherwise, things you really want to accomplish can get casually brushed aside.

Try setting appointments for untraditional things. Do you carry work worries home? If all other methods of shedding worry fail, simply allot yourself a "worry appointment" during which you have exactly 15 minutes to get the worry out of your system, then agree to move forward worry-free into your evening. Find yourself grazing throughout the day on unhealthy foods? Set a "junk food appointment" during which your cravings run free. (Rationale is around the corner folks . . .)

The idea behind this madness is that once these things become part of our to-do list, we will not want to do them as badly. Compare this concept to a story a general store owner once told me.

There was a vandal who would constantly graffiti his store's outside wall. As soon as the owner would paint over it, the vandal would turn around and "redecorate" with another masterpiece. The owner got a bright idea and posted a sign beside the wall that read: "To the graffiti artist: Having wall cleared tonight. Will pay you to paint my store's emblem." And you know what? To this day the wall is still white. The culprit never wreaked havoc again. Once their "art" became legitimate "work," they simply lost interest. You, too, will find that once your vices become "work," you will quickly lose interest.

This week set aside time for your behavioral flaws: worry, stress, pity-parties, and zone-out moments included. Once we slate appointments for these behaviors, we see how silly and time-consuming our actions can be. Soon you will likely decide they really don't belong on your to-do list after all.

● ● ● DISCUSSION 1 ● ● ●

What is something you once wanted to do so badly, but once you got around to it, it lost its appeal to you?

● ● ● DISCUSSION 2 ● ● ●

There is a saying that there is freedom in discipline. Just as we are creating "vice appointments" in this week's exercise, what is a creative system you have used in the past to drop a bad habit? How has this enriched the quality of your life?

Personal Dialogue

This part may be a little embarrassing, but list the top three "appointments" you would like to set for yourself. (Being mad at someone in your family, pouting about how much you make per year, etc.) After you're finished writing it out, how do you feel about making those "appointments"?

Keep an account of how your "appointments" went this week:

SUNDAY

MONDAY

TUESDAY

WEDNESDAY

THURSDAY

FRIDAY

SATURDAY

Be DefiANT

The story I'm about to share with you may read like an Aesop's fable. I assure you, however, that it is in fact a true animal kingdom story. (You can Google the pictures to prove it.) So everyone, gather 'round—it's story time.

One spring, there was a major storm that left acres of farm-land flooded. In those fields were mounds and mounds of ant colonies—colonies that were now underwater. But ants have proven to be resilient little creatures, and true to their deter-mined nature, they devised a plan.

All of the ants joined their little legs together and formed a living ant bridge. Their combined mass provided the needed buoyancy to float on the surface of the water. Once the ant bridge joined one area of dry land to another, one by one, the ants started walking across the living bridge to safety. Once back on land, those ants became busy moving the rest of the brood to a new mound in the making.

So here's the thing—when humans suffer a personal or collective crisis, let's say an economic downturn, rise in violence, political obstacle, or relationship deterioration, what do we do?

Panic. That's what we usually do.

Can you imagine how different **ALL** of our trials and tribulations would be if we defied the odds like ants do? In our flooding farmland fable, every condition points to the ants simply drowning. There is no human rescue team or government program to rally and help rebuild their colony. They figure it out and get to it—all on their own.

Let's reclaim our perseverance and power. You are not a victim to circumstance. You are only victim to how you *react* to circumstances.

Whatever trouble you may be facing today, look ahead to "dry land" and start taking steps to get there. The ants came to their own rescue and in just one afternoon laid the foundation for their new colony. Imagine what we humans can do in an entire day!

DISCUSSION 1

Sometimes we do find ourselves embodying the tenacity of the ant world—think of volunteer efforts after a natural disaster. How do you think we can personify that same "rally" attitude with other setbacks we face in the world?

DISCUSSION 2

It's hard not to give in to panic sometimes. It's almost easier to abandon rationale during a crisis than to harness and utilize it. But that's where having a plan is essential. When we are young, we practice fire drills so we reflexively know what to do should a real fire ever occur. Practicing drills actually keeps our minds focused on performing "the plan" rather than on having a free-for-all freak-out. Can you think of a time you executed a personal "plan" during an unnerving stage in your life? If not, think about a time you could have used a functional plan. Keep in mind that, like the ants, we possess a natural ability to persevere. Practice tapping into that vigor when predicaments emerge.

Personal Dialogue

There is a saying that perseverance, even more than skill set, is the key ingredient to success. In what areas of your life could use a greater measure of perseverance?

Keep an account of how you persevered despite the obstacles this week:

SUNDAY

MONDAY

TUESDAY

WEDNESDAY

THURSDAY

FRIDAY

SATURDAY

It's Okay to Not Know

Sitting around a coffee table, I listened to someone in her forties give one of the most honest answers I have ever heard to the "What is it you want to do?" career question. She smiled and said, "I really don't know. I have lots of passions, and I am good at many things but not excessively great at just *one* thing. I'm still trying to figure that one out myself!" I loved her for her candidness, and everyone at the table resonated with her statement.

The importance does not lie in *knowing* the answer but rather in being *open* to the answer.

Imagine being hungry and someone hands you an extensive menu of mouth-watering dishes to choose from that could satisfy your hunger. The catch is, you must make your selection **now!** You have only 30 seconds to make the call on your main entrée. The only thing you are sure of at that point is that you are hungry! The pressure then causes you to select the first thing that is familiar to you or that catches your eye. Had you been given sufficient time to consider each entrée, you may have arrived at a more desirable and satisfying conclusion.

Perhaps you are debating about a major, full-time career move, a belief system you can identify with, or the status of your relationship. There is no fault in not knowing certain elements in life. Being honest and open for the revelation to present itself is one of the ultimate favors you can do for yourself.

This week, shed the guilt of uncertainty and embrace your openness to sample life's expansive menu.

DISCUSSION 1

Being rushed is no fun. So why do we feel the need to rush ourselves and others into making important decisions in life? Remember when you learned to swim or ride a bike? It may have come easier to you or taken you a bit longer than some of your friends. Your mastery of either skill was dependent on a lot of different factors.

Can you think of an area in your life where you are currently on a learning curve and need to cut yourself some slack? Personal development is just that . . . development. It's a process. Growth takes place a step at a time thanks to your "life sampling" progress. You're never going to move from "not knowing" to "knowing" if you don't test some waters.

DISCUSSION 2

Why do you suppose our society pressures young people at such a young age to have their "act" together with regard to career, relationships, financial matters, personal demeanor— the whole shebang? At the same time, why do we question the rationality of anyone over 30 who is still trying to figure things out?

Personal Dialogue

We don't intend to, but we often judge the decisions of others based on how we would (or already did) respond to the same situation. When we expect others to live for our expectations, we aren't allowing them to form their own. Can you think of a time in your life when you just didn't know what to do? You actually wanted space to "not know" for a while? It is usually when we let go of the constant "What should I do?" loop that the answer emerges. What uncertainties are you ready to release in order to make peace with "not knowing"?

Keep an account of how you made peace with "not knowing" this week:

SUNDAY

MONDAY

TUESDAY

WEDNESDAY

THURSDAY

FRIDAY

SATURDAY

Quite Unnecessary

*"A teacher is one who makes himself
progressively unnecessary."*
—THOMAS CARRUTHERS

What do you think of that idea? When I first read it some time ago, I was confused by that rationale. My initial reaction was to be upset at the thought of being deemed "unnecessary." This whole idea seemed to conflict with my strong belief that we are each created because we are needed in some aspect. But after reading the quote again, it clicked— and I knew it was true.

The idea of being dispensable goes against our very nature. We're taught to stand out and advised to be irreplaceable. Yet this statement reminds us that we are not the be all and end all. My, how often we need to be reminded of that!

At one time, someone taught you. You absorbed that knowledge; it continues to be a part of who you are, and you pass that knowledge on to others. No matter what your role is in life, you are a teacher to someone. Lots of someones actually. Today, this week, and in *all* your future endeavors, remember that the goal is not for you to be the best and only ____ (fill in the blank). The goal is for you to authentically rise to that point in time when you can enthusiastically pass the torch to your enabled and empowered "students."

No one is immortal. But your unique influence will continue to spread far into the future—farther than you can imagine. For instance, we don't know who taught Michelangelo to paint, but we know he inspired countless others to pick up a paintbrush because of the passion and skill his teacher instilled in him. YOU play a vital role in the domino effect that will carry your acquired wisdom into generations to come.

When you embody your teacher role in life, you enable others to do the same elsewhere. If you could look at your life from an aerial view, you would see thousands of scattered students all across the world.

> *"A teacher affects eternity: he can never tell*
> *where his influence stops."*
> —Henry Adams

● ● ● DISCUSSION 1 ● ● ●

Fill in the blank: I am aspiring to be the best _____ I can be.
Now, how are you teaching others to be the best in that role as well? Who were your "teachers"?

● ● ● DISCUSSION 2 ● ● ●

The "looking out for number one" mentality drives people to succeed at all costs. But how sad to reach the top only to find you're all alone because you haven't invested time in caring for others along the way. When people embrace their "teacher" role on their way to the top, they can celebrate with their fellow travelers both along the journey and when they reach their summit. Think of various public figures that have been "teachers" to others who now have their own platforms. How rewarding to reach your goal while also being surrounded by the gratitude of others along the way!

Name some public figures (or people you know personally) whose students continue to promote their mission. (Examples: inventors, entertainers, artists, fitness icons, business moguls, athletes, etc.)

Personal Dialogue

Does it scare you to think of yourself as unnecessary? Perhaps it would be helpful to distinguish between "unnecessary" and "unwanted."

Recall when you were taught to tie your shoelaces. Did the person who taught you become "unwanted" after you learned to do it yourself? Chances are they were still just as wanted, but they were now unnecessary in your shoe-tying efforts. They were free to devote their energy to teaching you new things.

Think of some area of knowledge you may have been reluctant to pass on for fear that you would become unnecessary. Remember that when you pass the torch to others, you are essentially lighting your own pathway to discover new experiences and will repeat the sharing cycle.

Keep an account of how you embraced the "teacher" role in life this week:

SUNDAY

MONDAY

TUESDAY

WEDNESDAY

THURSDAY

FRIDAY

SATURDAY

No Camera?
No Problem

I had gotten a late start on my hike, so I ended up reaching the peak at exactly sunset, not the usual timing I would have planned for as I was unprepared for the dark descent. But life trumps our plan every time when it throws in the "Everything happens for a reason" card just at the right moment.

If I were an alien arriving on our planet during that sunset, I would have thought earth had an orange sky. Everything in my path took on the orange glow—the plants, the dirt path, and my own skin.

Then I looked to my left to find a completely different scene. As the sun was in the west, the moon was busy rising in the east. And it was a full moon at that. It's as if two skies had merged, and I was literally standing in the middle of day and night. It was amazing—a truly spiritual experience. I immediately thought, "I need to get a picture of this to send to so and so . . ." But in my rushed status, I had left everything behind at the house. It was a good thing I did.

Ironically, in that moment, I realized how many moments we miss trying to capture them. How many breathtaking experiences have you witnessed through a lens? Literally, think about that.

We all know a picture can't compare to the front row, so **why do we spend so much of our front-row time behind a lens?**

As an avid member of the memory-lapsing party, total recall is not my strong suit, so I totally get how photos are necessary to capture and relive certain moments that we want to revisit later down the road. But there is a balance. Try being fully present in the moment first. **When you receive the feeling that experience was meant to deliver to you, then go for the Kodak moment.** You'll find if you're primarily focused on capturing the moment for *later,* you'll miss the substance it wants to offer you in the *now.*

No camera, no problem. The deeply lived, "uncaptured" moments are just as meaningful as the photos you will share with friends. Just be in the moment, and let **it** capture **you**.

● ● ● DISCUSSION 1 ● ● ●

Sometimes our best moments happen when a camera is the furthest thing from our minds and we're too busy enjoying the moment to think about our devices. When was the last time you took in a "moment" without the aid of a camera?

● ● ● DISCUSSION 2 ● ● ●

What is your main intention when taking pictures? Is it to share the experience with others, to document occasions, or to reminisce with good memories on a rainy day? How often do you go back and look at the pictures you've collected over the years? (Perhaps plan a trip through a couple of old scrapbooks this week.)

Personal Dialogue

This week, make it a point to enjoy either a sunrise or sunset without any distractions (picture taking included). What eye-openers were revealed to you during this "moment"?

Keep an account of how you let your moments capture YOU this week:

SUNDAY

MONDAY

TUESDAY

WEDNESDAY

THURSDAY

FRIDAY

SATURDAY

A Stocked Shed

As I approached the age when many of my friends started to get married, I found much humor in watching my male friends undergo the engagement rituals. They put on their trooper pants for countless showers, photo sessions, wedding-planner consults, and family disputes. I think I got the biggest kick out of seeing how excited they each were for the "Tool and Gadget Party." As each gizmo was opened, you could see their mental wheels spinning around the countless projects that would be born as a result of their new "toys." After all, a shed is basically a grownup's fort.

Just as these newly engaged young men were gifted with all the items necessary for the well-stocked toolshed, we too are gifted with a world that is stocked in abundance with anything we could ever want or imagine. There are countless creeks and rivers, vast oceans, millions of plants and animals, shade, shelter, gorgeous views, and limitless variations of terrain to play on. We gain medicine, building materials, food, fuel, hobbies, and pets—all from Mother Nature's toolshed.

This week take a look in your toolbox (or desk organizer).

Note how each tool helps you accomplish a specific task. Study each utensil provided by the world around you with a sense of gratitude. We truly live in a stocked shed. Let's do what we can to keep it that way.

● ● ● DISCUSSION 1 ● ● ●

What are some of Mother Nature's tools that you are using at this very moment? (Example: sunlight, shade, air, wood, and clay for your home, etc.)

● ● ● DISCUSSION 2 ● ● ●

We keep our physical tools in a shed to protect them from the elements as well as to have an organized place to utilize them. Our national and state parks are one way we protect some of Mother Nature's tools so that the public can experience the wonders of nature within their confines. Likewise, as individuals, we need to protect our own inner tools, or assets, in some sort of refuge. Many people turn to faith practices, meditation, yoga, or prayer. Do you have a sacred space in which to protect your inner tools?

Personal Dialogue

Have you ever thought about how awesome it is that we were born into a "stocked shed"? Think of all of our modern marvels: skyscrapers, medicine, and transportation—all made from tools in Mother Nature's shed. Knowing that you were born into this world fully provided for, does this change any fear that you won't have "enough"? (Also refer to Week 2, "Spare Change.")

Keep an account of how you recognized and appreciated our planet's "stocked shed" this week:

SUNDAY

MONDAY

TUESDAY

WEDNESDAY

THURSDAY

FRIDAY

SATURDAY

Fresh Eye Effect

I am approaching my fourth year as a California resident, and I have decided that I may well be considered a tourist for the next 10 years. Every new part of town I discover is the greatest thing ever. Anything from a hiking trail or cozy restaurant to a new beach scene, coffee shop, park, or downtown destination is heaven on earth to me. I still get excited over the fact that I can see palm trees on my walk to the mailbox.

Throughout my "honeymoon" phase, I have paid special attention to the patience and accommodation granted by my friends who have lived here for years. If I want to backtrack for a picture, they oblige. If they have seen the ocean cliffs a hundred times, they still take me. They see the wonder I feel in my new element and give me the space and time to take it all in as a newcomer.

Maybe you are asked to rent a movie you have already seen, eat at a restaurant you visit frequently, vacation at a spot you have previously visited, or train the new hire . . . again. It is important to remember that while it may be routine or mundane for us, it is a completely new experience for someone else. **You have the privilege of being a part of their "first"—whatever it may be.**

This week, find satisfaction in being previously exposed to things that bring so much joy to newcomers. Allow yourself to see with fresh eyes, and enjoy the new life it can bring to old experiences.

● ● ● DISCUSSION 1 ● ● ●

When have you been granted patience concerning excitement you had toward something others had previously been exposed to?

● ● ● DISCUSSION 2 ● ● ●

Children are our best inspiration for seeing life with fresh eyes. After all, for the first couple of years of their life, everything *is* a new experience. Have you seen a toddler encounter a butterfly or a puppy for the first time? It's wonderful! Think about times when you witnessed a child have their first experience with something. How did it change how you viewed the experience yourself?

Personal Dialogue

Often we bypass a repeat experience because we want to see or do something new. Who doesn't love that first taste of a new experience? The thing to remember is, when you submit to a repeat experience for the sake of someone else, you receive the privilege of seeing the encounter through their eyes, which *is* a new experience in itself. What is something you have previously done, watched, or visited that you can share with someone you care about this week? Write about how introducing this experience to someone else made you feel.

Keep an account of how you looked at familiar experiences with fresh eyes this week:

SUNDAY

MONDAY

TUESDAY

WEDNESDAY

THURSDAY

FRIDAY

SATURDAY

Reality Bricks

A erial views are amazing in that they allow you to see things in their entirety. Your up-close-and-personal viewpoint suddenly transforms into "big picture" insight.

I was on a flight that hovered over a massive university library. One would think it held a small city due to its considerable size. The plane spent a good five minutes hovering over its architectural territory. It occurred to me that the library's construction workers must have felt at times as though they would never complete such an immense project. Years went into slowly turning a couple of bricks into a colossal structure.

It is important to remember that we encounter many construction projects in our life. There are periods when we start from scratch, some when we make additions, and some when we rebuild altogether. Discouragement in the initial stages is common and comes in many forms—unforeseen adverse circumstances, lack of a particular skill set, finances, help, or time. But you keep on laying the next brick and then the next. Slowly but surely, you will one day behold your own monumental accomplishment and marvel at how it grew from merely an idea into a wonderful reality.

This week, look at construction zones in a new light. It takes hundreds of workers to create a building or a stretch of road, just as hundreds of people will come into play assisting you toward your goals. Have patience with setbacks and unforeseen obstacles. One brick at a time, you will build your reality.

DISCUSSION 1

What is the most amazing structure you have witnessed in its entirety? How long do you estimate it took to manifest from start to finish? What thoughts ran through your head as you took it all in?

DISCUSSION 2

A fun thing to do is think of people in your support circle as your construction crew, the very folks that help you design and implement your life goals. Who makes up your construction crew and what are their roles?

Personal Dialogue

We often show impatience toward construction workers when we see them "standing around." How often do you "stand around" your own construction site? Let this admission provide tolerance for future individuals you believe are just "standing around" as well as motivate you to roll up your sleeves and get on with your own life projects.

Keep an account of how you admired and activated the construction zones in your life this week:

SUNDAY

MONDAY

TUESDAY

WEDNESDAY

THURSDAY

FRIDAY

SATURDAY

Earth as a Moon

I recently enjoyed a theatrical performance that illustrated the earth as a moon. The characters danced on a foreign planet while the earth cast its shadow overhead. It was a beautiful metaphor with a stirring message: what we are exposed to shapes our reality. If I had asked a character in the play to point at the moon, they would have pointed to what I call earth.

Our individual views in life operate by the same principle. While you grew up believing something as an absolute truth, someone sharing a different perspective grew up declaring a different version of that truth. Suppose someone going through a difficult situation asked you, "What should I do to make this better?" Your response would reflect the beliefs you held because of what you were exposed to. The person who grew up in a different culture or even just in a different family may offer an opposite view of what the person should do to improve their situation.

Instead of wasting time debating whose advice angle is correct, why not look at the bigger picture? Make room for the possibility that someone else's understanding might be just as valid as our own. Our "earth" just may be someone else's "moon." The prevailing realization here is that, in our own unique way, each of us reflects the *same* Sun. Regardless of our perspectives and opinions, we all contain the same Light.

This week, regardless if people share our views, acknowledge that they do share the same experience as human beings making their way—just from a different perspective. Instead of concentrating on our different definitions of life, focus on the Light we all have in common.

DISCUSSION 1

When you meet friends, you generally connect around what you have in common. Think of someone in your life who has a different philosophy than you do. What are the traits you have in common with them?

DISCUSSION 2

Have you ever been involved in an argument in which you were *certain* you were right, only to be proven wrong? Care to fess up to your blunder tale? Remember that sensation when you prejudge different viewpoints. Just because we're convinced we are right, doesn't mean we are.

Personal Dialogue

Beliefs are meaningful to us because they define how we live our lives. Each person has an intimate relationship with their

particular philosophies. Imagine you were a character in the play mentioned earlier, would you have picked an argument with one of the people who thought earth was actually a moon? Or would you have said, "Interesting, I actually call earth a planet. Do you want to know what that is?"

Keep an account of how you respected others' various "moons" this week:

SUNDAY

MONDAY

TUESDAY

WEDNESDAY

THURSDAY

FRIDAY

SATURDAY

Living Water

Water is the simplest and yet most complex element on earth. It is strong, yet gentle. It can be fog, humidity, ice, sweat, a cool puddle, or a boiling geyser. While it has many forms, its components remain the same regardless of the identity it assumes.

Water is the most abundant molecule in the human body. Just as water uses its components to form various identities, your body taps into its elemental ability to withstand the many different experiences life will present you. You will morph from a carefree adolescent to a young adult, an individual to a partner, a companion to a parent, a recipient of help to the giver of help, and a person with questions to someone with answers. Throughout each transformation, you essentially remain the same despite surface appearance.

This week, with each drink of water, connect with part of your identity. What transformation led to the current role you primarily embody? Do you feel as if any secondary roles are in transition?

● ● ● DISCUSSION 1 ● ● ●

Water has countless uses depending on any given circumstance. We can wash our bodies and clothes with it, drink it, or cook in it. When we think of all the circumstances in our lives and how they have moved us into different forms or roles, we realize what a wide array of capabilities we have cultivated. We are useful in many ways we probably never would have imagined. What are some areas in which you have become quite proficient as you've moved through your various forms/roles in life thus far?

● ● ● DISCUSSION 2 ● ● ●

Water is essential—our life source. Without it, nothing would survive on earth. What "water"/ life force do you draw from? How does that transition into different forms? (Example: if family is your life force, it could morph from your immediate family, to your friendships as a young adult, to your own young family, and back again to a small group of friends once the nest is empty.)

Personal Dialogue

Just because water happens to be ice, doesn't mean it will always remain in that state. Factors such as the sun or exposure to other elements can cause ice to turn into a puddle rather quickly. Likewise, whatever phase we now find ourselves in can change in a moment. How can you open yourself up to all you are meant to encounter in this current phase?

Keep an account of how you embraced your current form this week:

SUNDAY

MONDAY

TUESDAY

WEDNESDAY

THURSDAY

FRIDAY

SATURDAY

Pining for
a Difference?

A mini-excursion into the mountains presented me with a new look at an old friend: the pine tree. Passing row after row after row of pine trees, I fought the urge to fall into a sleepy hypnotic trance. I vowed I would be a good passenger and at least keep the driver company until a decent radio signal came in and I could conk out free of guilt.

Thus the gates of Memory Lane flung open as I recalled my family searching through rows and rows of pine trees for the perfect Christmas tree each year. We'd eagerly get it home, decorate it, and embark upon the *Fa La La* of the season as we knew it.

Shortly after the advent of the season, like clockwork, I would always get sick. Tissue boxes adorned every room as I sneezed, coughed, and blew through my annual affliction. Mom or Dad could always count on missing a holiday gathering of some kind because I was cold-ridden.

It wasn't until I was about 12 years old that we finally figured out I was allergic to pine trees. All those years we thought I was susceptible to colds around the holidays when I was really sharing living quarters with the culprit. It got me thinking about how often innocent factors in life get a bad wrap when the guilty party to blame is right there—*under our nose.*

Perhaps you are down in the dumps and pointing the finger at a job, someone else's behavior, or a financial hurdle. It is easy to try to place blame, but a closer look could reveal your actual funk lies elsewhere. On top of that, it could be a funk you *invited* in. Did you ask for more stress when you said you'd take on another client, carpool, or project? Perhaps your unwise spending invites panic at the end of each month. Or you could be doing the right job, just at the wrong place.

Many times you'll find the source of your tizzy has been right in front of you all along. In my case, I not only helped my family select it and opened my doors to it, I hung around it every day. You might actually find your culprit receives like treatment.

> *"The people and circumstances around me*
> *do not make me what I am; they reveal who I am."*
> —LAURA SCHLESSINGER

●　●　● **DISCUSSION 1** ●　●　●

The interesting thing about this story is the pine tree was never really doing anything wrong . . . it was only being itself, after all. It was the fact that it was taken out of its natural setting and added to MY natural setting in an unnatural way. What are some situations in your life that may be uncomfortable or even painful because one or more people are not in their usual environment?

● ● ● DISCUSSION 2 ● ● ●

Have you been playing the blame game with regard to certain obstacles you've been facing? Are you ready to identify the real culprits? Release the tension that blaming causes and think of productive measures to move toward a solution. When we take responsibility for the error, we can responsibly make a change.

For example: You have been blaming your sister for your tight budget each month due to lending her money—and you don't even approve of how she is spending it. The blame in this situation actually lies in your own boundary setting. Sit and write about what boundaries and stipulations you genuinely feel comfortable with moving forward, and replace feelings of animosity with feelings of gratitude that you have the means to offer such assistance.

Personal Dialogue

Think of a time you were unrightfully blamed for someone's problems. How did it make you feel? How can you apply that feeling to future encounters where your finger wants to do some pointing?

Keep an account of how you proactively identified the REAL culprits at the core of your issues this week:

SUNDAY

MONDAY

TUESDAY

WEDNESDAY

THURSDAY

FRIDAY

SATURDAY

The Idea of the Idea

everal years ago, one of my personal projects was to learn to play the guitar. I grew up listening to my dad play and saw the joy simply pulling out the guitar case gave him. He lit up and would strum through different chords for hours. As you know, joy follows joy, and my sister and I would don our tutus, lace gloves, and plastic heels as we'd dance and sing along with dad's mini-concert in our bedroom. As I grew into a writer, I thought putting my words and ideas into song was the perfect marriage. I had the lyric part down. Now to put those words to a melody with chords . . . thus the guitar light bulb switched on.

I received a shiny guitar for my 21st birthday and vowed to know how to play by my dad's birthday (which was 6 months away). I printed off chords, took tutorials, and plugged away at the guitar for months and months. The thing was, I found that I never looked forward to pulling out my guitar case. In fact, I dreaded it. I didn't particularly care to learn the bazillion different chords and found the transition to those bazillion different chords rather frustrating. One day I had to get real with myself. Was I getting lazy and discouraged with something I genuinely loved or **was I simply in love with an idea** and facing the repercussions of chasing the illusion surrounding that idea?

In my self-analysis, I discovered I was in fact in love with the idea of an idea. I correlated the happy and memorable times with my dad as a kid with playing the guitar. **A musical instrument didn't cause that joy. My dad taking part in what gave him joy caused that joy.** I could play the guitar all day long and no one would get that feel-good, joyful vibe because I don't genuinely love playing like my dad did.

Now, give me a pen and paper and time to write a story, and I will work a room with my imagination. That is my pure, complete joy. With that revelation out in the open, I happily sold my guitar to a man dying to get hold of that exact model. I have no doubt rooms are filled with amusement and liveliness due to the love and excitement he puts into his music.

Are you currently grinding away at a project, career, or relationship that you think will give you certain results based on an idea? Many good-intentioned individuals pursue happiness based on an idea that worked for someone else but doesn't quite register a chord with their own being. Is this idea propelling you into something that your heart just really isn't in? If you find you're not actually as happy as you thought you would be, check in with yourself.

Here's to making music in your own loving way.

● ● ● DISCUSSION 1 ● ● ●

Can you think of a fun memory that was made because someone else was pursuing their passions? (For example: You attended an amazing football game because your friend was the coach and hooked you up!) Did that particular experience inspire you in any way?

DISCUSSION 2

Perhaps you are someone people frequently want to "tap into" when it comes to that joyful vibe. How can you encourage others to pursue their passions in order to cultivate their own personal "spark"?

Personal Dialogue

Perhaps you can think of something you have pursued because you fell in love with a particular idea. One way to distinguish whether you are avoiding discipline or are truly pursuing the wrong path to ask yourself, "If circumstances were neither good nor bad (at a neutral), would I have joy in this pursuit or more questions and doubts?"

Keep an account this week of how you were able to distinguish between pursuing a passion and pursuing an idea:

SUNDAY

MONDAY

TUESDAY

WEDNESDAY

THURSDAY

FRIDAY

SATURDAY

Water Break

I had just received my receipt from the cashier and decided to head outside to soak up some sun while I waited for my order. The cashier's little girl was seated on the steps entertaining herself during her "go to work with mom" day. She was as cute as could be in her sparkly sneakers and bubbling over with endless topics of conversation. I was amused to learn all about her dog's birthday celebrations and her kindergarten teacher.

Directly behind us, her brother was with some friends attempting skateboard tricks. I felt like I was back on summer break and planning my next slumber party. Abruptly, my new mini-friend declared, "I'm thirsty. I'm going to get some water." And I watched her march inside and pour herself a plastic cup full.

It was just a few minutes later that her brother kicked up the skateboard and decided he was thirsty too. Rather than hitting the cooler as his little sister had done, he went inside where his mom was busy with orders and asked, "Mom, can I have some water?"

I'm not sure if it's conditioning from how you were raised or your own inborn gumption, but some of us go get the water and some of us ask for it.

Maybe you're experiencing a desire for something right now, and you're going through the asking process. You're asking for permission, approval, or think you need a particular person's guidance to get there.

It's yours for the taking. Just go get it.

DISCUSSION 1

Are you more of a "seize the opportunity" or an "ask for the opportunity" kind of person? Do you believe you were conditioned to be this way? List examples of experiences that gave you either the gumption and gusto trait or the permission-slip approach to life.

DISCUSSION 2

What is something you want in your life that you've relied on others to make happen for you? What action step can you perform this week to put yourself at the control center of making that happen?

Personal Dialogue

Gumption is a talent just like any other skill set. Each of our personal capabilities takes practice. Try rehearsing a scenario in which you would like to conduct yourself with more confidence and gumption. (A partner or a mirror works.)

Keep an account of how you stepped into your gumption this week:

SUNDAY

MONDAY

TUESDAY

WEDNESDAY

THURSDAY

FRIDAY

SATURDAY

Roots on a Rock

Ever notice a tree growing from a cliff or a flower blooming perfectly from the middle of a sidewalk? If you turn to garden experts or farmers, you'll hear how plants need nutrients and ideal conditions to truly flourish. However, these plants growing in the most unlikely of places seem to prove that there are exceptions to this theory.

This phenomenon can also apply to our personal growth. It would seem that the perfect environment to develop into a sound adult would be one characterized by constant love, support, stability, adequate finances, and physical nourishment. In reality, many of us grow up without these ideal conditions, and yet life goes on. And so does our growth. Despite less-than-perfect upbringings and circumstances, we have the power to learn through our obstacles and grow into the people we want to be.

We are inspired when we hear about people who rose above their troublesome circumstances to achieve great things—someone with a disability becoming a superior athlete, a child raised with both parents in jail becoming a political leader, or a young woman abused as a child becoming a loving mom to a house full of kids. Despite their rocky conditions, they still lived life in full bloom. They are the human examples of thriving flowers amidst rough terrain.

There's no harm in having or striving for favorable growing conditions, but we live in a dynamic world—not in a controlled greenhouse. Next time you go on a hike or pass a rocky terrain, notice the multitude of plant life rooted in rock and let it renew your faith in the strength of your own root system. Our growth process will no doubt face times where we lack vital components to reach our potential, but let our powerful foliage friends symbolize our own inner resilience.

DISCUSSION 1

What achievements have you attained after overcoming difficult circumstances?

DISCUSSION 2

What current hardship are you facing? How can you apply what you learned about yourself in Discussion 1 to this circumstance?

Personal Dialogue

This week, take special note of *anything* you see that is thriving in adverse conditions. (For example: the sweet demeanor of a child at a department store despite their parent's objectionable behavior or your single parent coworker's resolve to make family dinners and the kids' sporting events happen.) Let it bring some pep to your step knowing you have that same power to rise above your circumstances and bloom beautifully.

Keep an account of how you flourished amidst rocky conditions this week:

SUNDAY

MONDAY

TUESDAY

WEDNESDAY

THURSDAY

FRIDAY

SATURDAY

This is not the end.

Only the preface to your new beginning.

I hope you feel emotionally lifted from your positivity sessions and found candid clarity in your discoveries. I encourage you to continue seeking material that raises questions for conscious answers.

> *"The way life treats you is a mirror image*
> *of your attitude towards life."*
> —UNKNOWN

Interested in starting your own *Week to Strong* book club? Visit katcowley.com for details.

About the Author

Author and workshop creator **Kat Cowley** loves giving Personal Development a personal touch. Humble life metaphors are her teachers of choice. Her greatest joy throughout all of her work is to see people form a tangible relationship with a new way of thinking because they were introduced to an impactful illustration.

For more information, please visit www.katcowley.com.